HOW MUCH MORE

ROBERT GORDON

Merry Christmas, Mark:
I pray that this book
would be an encouragement
and inspiration to you

In Christ,

Danny

Marshalls

Marshalls Paperbacks
Marshall Morgan & Scott

3 Beggarwood Lane, Basingstoke, Hants.

Copyright © Robert Gordon 1983
First published by Marshall Morgan & Scott 1983

Bible references are from the New International
Version, except where indicated.

ISBN 0 551 01034 7

Printed in Great Britain by
Hunt Barnard Printing Ltd., Aylesbury, Bucks.

To my wife Hilda

and Jonathan our son

who share with me

in the love and joy of Jesus

Acknowledgements

The body of Christ is more then mere doctrine, it is a living fact!

I am grateful to God for that part of the Body which is the Bethany fellowship and all that that means in terms of support, encouragement, and, at times, correction. We all need each other in the love of Jesus!

In particular, I want to thank Katie, Jo, Paul, Hilary and Barbara, members of my own team and household without whose love and help this book would never have been written.

It is hardly possible to put into words all that is gained from sharing life and ministry with my fellow elders and partners in the Gospel; Colin, Charles, David and Michael.

Contents

Preface

I found myself asking what difference it had made.

Ten years ago I was minister of a United Reformed Church in Durham and chaplain within the University of Durham. My earlier Christian background had been in the Plymouth Brethren in the west of Scotland and later in England. It had become increasingly clear to me, involved as I was in the lives of many young people, that my background and my theological training had left me ill-equipped to deal with the problems and questions with which I was being confronted.

I suffered from power-failure. I seemed to lack the ability to get what I believed about God and his love out of my head and into the lives of those people who most desperately needed something. The result, for me, was a long period of inward agony and spiritual search which often brought with it periods of darkness and doubt too deep for words.

It was out of this situation that the events and insights of this book were born. As a result of the experience related in the first chapter, I discovered a whole new dimension of Christian experience. God became real, his word began to live for me, and I discovered a new power at the centre of my work and ministry.

In the years that have passed since then, I have come more and more to recognise that experience as something of great significance. It has had results not only within the confines of my own life and family but far beyond in the lives of many other people. It has changed the whole shape of my life and ministry. It has led me now to believe that the results of such an experience of God are radically important, not only for one individual, but for the life of the whole Church and its witness in the world.

This book is the outcome of my opening question. It is an

attempt to share something of the difference the experience has made and goes on making. It can only be a partial answer because it is one individual's experience, but I pray that it will be a stimulating answer which will prompt others to seek the reality of God for themselves.

1: Encounter with God

'In the year that King Uzziah died, I saw the Lord seated on a throne, high and exalted, and the train of his robe filled the temple' (Isaiah 6.1).

Our experience of God colours everything else in our Christian lives. How we know God and what we know about him will determine the way we live.

There was something missing in my own experience of God. I had understood him in terms of his love for me in Jesus. I appreciated what he had done for me through the death and resurrection of Jesus. I knew something, in my mind at least, of the nature of God as it is revealed to us through the writings of the Old and New Testaments. Yet there was still something missing.

There was a certain lack of reality. It was almost as though God was experienced at second-hand. It was not that I did not believe in him. After all, I was an ordained minister of the United Reformed Church who had vowed to proclaim his word and administer his sacraments. It was not that I had no commitment. For the past eighteen years or more I had lived consciously as a Christian and, when the time had come, had given up the prospect of a lucrative future in business to answer the call to the ministry.

That was all to be changed within the space of twelve hours. It actually took more than two years, but, in the end, a new awareness of God broke through like a sudden burst of sunshine on a cloudy day.

For almost two and a half years I had been a chaplain within the University of Durham and minister of a city-centre church. I became increasingly aware of the need for a greater freedom and power at the heart of my own ministry. The problems I was meeting in the lives of many students were not going to be solved by a dissertation on Christian doctrine. The students needed a touch of God's power in their lives and for that to happen to them something needed to happen to me!

In the spring of 1974 I found myself at a special conference for clergy run by the Fountain Trust at a place called Carberry Towers. An invitation from a fellow minister and friend had drawn me there filled with apprehension and suspicion about some of the things I imagined I might find.

Nothing happened as far as I was concerned until the last night. An Anglican priest was speaking from Isaiah chapter 6 about the reality and holiness of God. When the meeting finished everybody left and went downstairs for supper but I found myself unable to move out of my chair. A great dark cloud of heaviness and depression seemed to have settled on my head. For the first time almost in my whole Christian experience I felt as though I had been face to face with a man through whom the reality of God was shining. It left me with a feeling of utter hopelessness and a deep sense of sin. I felt absolutely desolate and completely broken in spirit.

The words of Isaiah 6 seemed entirely appropriate at that moment:

"'Woe to me!' I cried. 'I am ruined! For I am a man of unclean lips'" (Isaiah 6.5).

A short time passed before my friends realised that I had not gone down to supper. Two of them came back upstairs to find me sitting in the chair. They said very little. It was almost as though they understood what was happening. They very quietly laid their hands on my head and prayed with me. I know nothing of the words of that prayer but recall its effect: I felt shaky and trembled as though I had just had a near miss in a car accident. It was like that when I went to bed, but when I woke the next morning I felt as though the sun had risen in my spirit rather than in the sky.

The reality of that experience has never left me. It gave me a completely new perspective on God and changed the course of my ministry. I felt as though I had met both the holiness of God and his restoring forgiveness.

10

Recently I came across a verse in the apocryphal book of Ecclesiasticus. It puts into a nutshell what is, for me, this experience of the reality of God:

'As his majesty is, so too is his mercy' (Ecclesiasticus 2.23, Jerusalem Bible).

The heart of the Holy Spirit's work is to reveal God to us. Many other things may happen to us as part of the Spirit's working in our lives, but at the centre there needs to be this 'God-awareness'. We may gain the ability to speak with another tongue, or the power to prophesy, or the gift of healing, but, unless we experience this reality of God the rest will soon evaporate or become distorted and self-centred.

P. T. Forsyth, a Congregational writer at the beginning of this century, said that 'a gospel that goes deep enough has all the breadth in the world that it needs.' If renewal is to mean anything for keeps in the Church today then it must start and finish with God. The Holy Spirit is God expounding himself within the realm of my experience.

There are certain important parts to that experience which make it so vital to our lives.

1. It is an experience of the holiness of God

The most astounding thing to discover about holiness is that it is not a set of rules and regulations.

Holiness is not trying to be good. Holiness is an encounter. It is a meeting, in a personal way, with God as he is. To feel the impact of God's presence in that way is to begin to understand why Jacob and Moses and many other ancient men and women of God recoiled from the presence of the divine:

'It is a dreadful thing to fall into the hands of the living God' (Hebrews 10.31).

'Holy' is what God is. The root of the word in Hebrew means 'to separate' or 'to be separate'. The main idea with regard to God is not that he is distant from man but that he is distinct from man in his nature. Whereas we are impure in our thoughts and actions, he is pure. Whereas we are mortal, he is immortal. Everything that we are on the negative side, God is not. It is summed up in the words of Hosea the prophet:

'I am God and not man – the Holy One among you' (Hosea 11.9).

The other great reality of the Old Testament that goes along with 'holiness' is 'glory'. 'Glory' is what happens when God decides to show himself within the realm of man's experience. Every time we read of God being present in some way there is mention of 'glory'. There was fire and smoke on top of the mountain when the law was given and the glory of the Lord appeared. Smoke filled the house at the dedication of the temple in the time of Solomon and the glory of the Lord filled the place. In the experience of Isaiah the same glory was seen:

'Holy, holy, holy is the Lord Almighty; the whole earth is full of his glory' (Isaiah 6.3).

The title 'the Holy One of Israel' occurs no less than twenty six times within the book of Isaiah.

It was this experience of the holiness of God that was the foundation of Isaiah's message. It is this understanding of the holiness of God that stands at the heart of all that the Old Testament has to say about God. It is this holiness of God that is revealed above all in the life and teaching of Jesus:

'We have seen his glory, the glory of the one and only Son, who came from the Father, full of grace and truth' (John 1.14).

It is this holiness that we are called to share through the work of the Holy Spirit within our lives. As the Spirit makes us aware of who God is, we feel the impact of his presence within us:

'And we, who with unveiled faces all reflect the Lord's glory, are being transformed into his likeness with ever-increasing glory, which comes from the Lord, who is the Spirit' (2 Corinthians 3.18).

In some deep and challenging words, P. T. Forsyth highlights the importance of this experience of holiness to our Christian lives:

'This holiness of God is the real foundation of religion: love is but its outgoing; sin is but its defiance; grace is but its action on sin; the Cross is but its victory; faith is but its worship.'

If 'holy' is what God is, then holiness must stand at the centre of every real experience of renewal. It is this experience of the holiness of God that causes us to turn away (for that is what repentance really means) from ourselves and everything in our lives that is opposed to the goodness of God. After all, it is not so much *renewal* we need as *restoration*. We need to be restored in the power of the Holy Spirit to all that God meant us to be when he created man in the first instance. It was disobedience and pride that took man away from that divine image. What is happening when the Holy Spirit begins to do his work is that he is restoring us to the image of our creator: Pentecost is the recovery of what was lost in the Fall.

It takes a personal relationship with God to restore that image. It was this personal relationship that was broken because of Adam's sin.

It should come as no surprise that this experience of the holiness of God will not, in the first instance, be a happy one. The result of being aware of God as he really is is total dislocation of the inner being. The description that Isaiah gives of his own experience of God is something that is true to the experience of every human being who has travelled this way. This was the missing link, as far as I was concerned, in all my evangelical religion. I had been taught about the holiness of God, and I had preached about the holiness of God, but I had never experienced the holiness of God!

The complete darkness of spirit and disorientation of mind that results from being confronted by the holiness of God is something from which a person can never fully recover. It is like the meeting that Jacob had with God at the brook called Jabbok (Genesis chapter 32). Jacob was restored by God and was a new man after that, but he bore in his body for ever after the marks of his meeting with God. That encounter with the holiness of God not only determined the direction of Jacob's life but the lives of countless thousands of generations after him. It is in this sort of context that we need to see what God is doing in our lives today. It is important for us, but it is not important only for us. How we respond to God may well be important for many other people after us.

God uses many means to bring us to that point of encounter. In my own case he hounded my footsteps for more than two years. He brought me out of the shell of my own sufficiency into a deep experience of despair and agony. He needed to bring me to a point of breaking within my spirit.

One of the chief things that God used as a challenge was the testimony of an Anglican priest who himself had once been a university chaplain before teaching theology in one of the major Scottish universities. His name is Roland Walls. We invited him to speak at a conference for university chaplains to be held in Durham where I was. What he had to say affected me very deeply.

He spoke of his own experience of dereliction, of how there came a point in his work and ministry at which he realised that God was not real for him in a personal way. He knew nothing of the power of God within the practice of his faith. Although he had been a priest and teacher for many years, he felt completely desolate and empty. In his despair he decided to go south to visit an old friend and spiritual confidant. He caught a night train from Edinburgh but the further south he travelled the more depressed in spirit he became. He asked God to say something to him that would help his despair. At that moment, as he was sitting looking out of the compartment window, a goods train came the other way. He watched it go past his window wagon by wagon. Then an amazing thing happened! The last wagon came into view and chalked on the side of it were some words of instruction to the shunt-yard workmen. In bold letters it proclaimed, 'Return Empty to Scotland!' Those words became God's word to Roland Walls. He did just that. He got off the train and caught the next train back to Scotland, where he discovered new life in God through an experience of being filled with the Holy Spirit.

I recognised in the testimony of that man echoes of my own search: the same desolation of spirit and restlessness in ministry and the same desire to find something that went deeper than all that I had known in my previous religious life.

God used that testimony to deepen my awareness and finally to open me to the same challenge of the Spirit for myself.

Without an awareness of the holiness of God we are in danger of having renewal without reformation. The work of the Holy Spirit is not to introduce the Church of the twentieth century to yet another novel cultural expression of the faith. No doubt when we follow the leading of the Spirit we will find that many of our cherished traditions will seem pointless and will need to go, but at its heart, renewal by the Spirit is about restoration into the image of God. It is this 'God-awareness' that is central to any real experience of renewal by the Holy Spirit. What I came face to face with for the first time at Carberry Towers was the holiness of God:

'My ears had heard of you
but now my eyes have seen you.
Therefore I despise myself and repent in
dust and ashes' (Job 42. 5, 6).

2. It is an experience of the forgiveness of God

The verse that I found in Ecclesiasticus highlights a tremendous spiritual truth:

'As his majesty is, so too is his mercy'.

To experience the holiness of God is to have become aware of the majesty of God. It is something that cannot finally be put into words. Those who have no inkling in their own experience of what Isaiah is speaking about often view him as nothing other than a profound poet of the Jewish tradition, but Isaiah was expressing in his own way what we all need to find for ourselves.

There is only one thing in the world as great as the majesty of God and that is his mercy! The writer of Psalm 103 knew exactly the same thing:

'Praise the Lord, O my soul:
all my inmost being, praise his holy name . . .

He does not treat us as our sins deserve
or repay us according to our iniquities.

For as high as the heavens are above the
earth, so great is his love for those who
fear him' (Psalm 103. 1,10,11).

If we were left only with the awful awareness of God's
holiness then we would be left in dust and ashes within our
spirits, but Isaiah's experience of the forgiveness of God is
true to every real experience of the Holy Spirit. If we are
broken by God, it is for our healing. Indeed, we may say that
it is not until we have been really broken before God that we
can experience healing. Until he deals with those things in our
lives that stand opposed to his rule and will, we cannot know
the full freedom of living in relationship with him.

The effect of forgiveness within our lives cannot be over
estimated. To live in the good of what God has done for us in
Jesus is to know in our daily living the freedom that belongs to
those who have experienced his cleansing. Many people
believe that Jesus died for them and live in the hope of
ultimate salvation but they live their present lives under a
cloud of guilt, imprisoned by feelings and circumstances
which hold them under control. We need a touch of God's
Spirit which will enable us to live in the reality of what Paul
speaks about in Romans chapter 8:

'Therefore, there is now no condemnation for those who
are in Christ Jesus, because through Christ Jesus the
law of the Spirit of life set me free from the law of sin
and death' (Romans 8. 1, 2).

The word translated 'condemnation' in our English
versions is an interesting word. It is the word that was used
for the sentence a prisoner had to serve after being found
guilty of a particular offence. In this case it meant a sentence
of hard labour, a lifetime of penal servitude. After a trial the
verdict is passed: Guilty or Not Guilty. Then, if the
defendant is found Guilty, the sentence is given. What the
Devil tries to do within our lives is to see to it that, although
we believe our guilt has been removed through the sacrifice of
Jesus, we still live as though we were serving a sentence of
hard labour. For years I never saw the full import of the
words of Wesley:

'He breaks the power of cancelled sin,
He sets the prisoner free.
His blood can make the foulest clean,
His blood availed for me.'

At the human level, of course, there appear to be good grounds for feeling despair. There are a number of factors which prevent us from living in the freedom of the Spirit:

(a) *There is the tension that arises between the opposite sides of our character*

Every one of us feels the tension that the Apostle Paul expresses so clearly in Romans chapter 7. Time and again we experience the frustration of being the kind of people we are. The struggle that goes on within us, between our longings to do good and our tendency towards evil, threatens to overwhelm any possibility of things being different.

'I do not understand what I do. For what I want to do I do not do, but what I hate I do. . . . What a wretched man I am! Who will rescue me from this body of death?' (Romans 7. 15, 24).

Not long ago I saw a Snoopy cartoon in which the little dog was lying on top of his kennel in a very philosophical mood. His nose drooped over the end of the hut and the caption above his head said it all:

'Yesterday I was a dog, today I am a dog, tomorrow I'll be a dog. I see little room for advancement.'

The Devil can be a great realist when he wants to be. There are occasions when he wants us to know all the true facts about ourselves. He knows that if we face things as they actually are at the human level the result will be despair and hopelessness in our hearts. It takes the power of the Holy Spirit to release us from that kind of bondage.

(b) *There is the recollection of past failures*

Some time ago we were leading a mission. During that week

17

we met one Christian who had been living in depression for some months. Something had happened in her life over which she had no control and it had created a deep guilt complex in her mind, so much so that she could not rid herself of the thought of that wrong. She could not escape the bondage it had brought into her life.

The past can wield a powerful sway within our experience. The future we fear but pray that when it comes we will be able to deal with it. In the present we muddle through, often pretending that things are not as bad as they are. The past, however, is gone for ever and yet its events and circumstances often seem able to hold us in their grip.

Sometimes we discover the power of the past in the same way that we discover memories during a spring-clean. As we look into corners that haven't been disturbed for a long time we find articles from long ago and every one of them carries its own story. Sometimes we don't finish the cleaning because of the memories!

It's like that in spiritual terms. The Devil has a good rake around in our spiritual attics and he finds things there that seemed dead and gone. Then we discover that the events and sins of yesterday have a pretty powerful hold today. Suddenly it seems that all our achievements over the years as a Christian mean nothing and memories from the past fetter the present with guilt.

It takes the Holy Spirit to break the power of that chain. As I spoke with that young woman in the mission God put a picture into my mind. It was a picture of how he looks at our lives. We see them a bit at a time because we live moment by moment. For us the future has not yet been and the past is without recall. With God it is different. He stands outside our time-scale. He views our lives as a whole and there is no part of that whole which is not present to him.

That is a very significant fact because it means that there is no point within the scale of my life that God cannot touch. He can bring healing to me in this moment from the things I lived through yesterday!

Wasn't it Corrie Ten Boom who made that well-known version of Micah 7. 19?

'He has taken all my sins and cast them into the depths

of the sea, and on the shore he has posted a notice that says, "No Fishing"!'

(c) *There is the realisation of our need*

Sometimes the thing that keeps us from knowing God's deliverance is the recognition of how very great our need is. Indeed, so great does our need appear to us that it seems too enormous for God to do anything about.

I was called to speak with a woman one night at the end of a meeting. Other team members had spoken with her, but felt, in the end, that I should see her. She seemed to betray absolutely no emotion and when I spoke with her it became clear that although she desperately wanted help she was almost overwhelmed by the immensity of her problems.

Twenty-five years before, she and her husband had separated. It had caused her such great hurt that she had decided there and then that she would never again risk being in such a vulnerable situation. So she had cut herself off emotionally from every other person, protecting her spirit by withdrawing deep inside herself. Of course, what happened was that she herself suffered more than anyone else. There she was, completely frozen in herself, and quite overwhelmed by the size of the problem she had created.

As I prayed with her God gave me a vivid picture of the protective cage she had built. I could almost see it enveloping her body. As I laid my hands on her head to pray for her I could feel her recoiling from the touch. I prayed with the words of Romans 5.5:

'God has poured out his love into our hearts by the Holy Spirit, whom he has given us.'

The effect was dramatic. It was almost as though someone had come with a large key and had turned it in the padlock that was holding the cage. I could almost see the cage being lifted away. She began to cry for the first time in many years. Then the joy of Jesus touched her heart and she found a new release in the power of God. She had been forgiven. She had forgiven herself and she found in her heart a new power to forgive the person who had caused her that hurt all those years before.

The forgiveness of God is a very powerful agent. It is that touch of God's Spirit that stands at the heart of the experience of Isaiah the prophet:

> 'Then one of the seraphs flew to me with a live coal in his hand, which he had taken with tongs from the altar. With it he touched my mouth and said. "See, this has touched your lips; your guilt is taken away and your sin atoned for"' (Isaiah 6.6).

These words may seem, to those who don't know for themselves the power of forgiveness, merely a beautiful poetic expression of some deep mystical experience of the prophet, but for those who know the power of forgiveness they are the apt expression of the spirit of a man who has discovered for himself the cleansing mercy of God.

3. It is an experience of the call of God

The rest of this book is, in some senses, an exposition of what this encounter with God has meant for me. If we stay with the experience of Isaiah for a moment longer we will see that what he came to know of the holiness of God and the measure to which he experienced the grace of God, were but introductions to the real reason for both these things. God wanted to use him!

Again it was some words of P. T. Forsyth that made their point about this in my own mind:

> 'Now we come to the practical point . . . what is the effect of God's mercy upon your life? You believe in the mercy of God; how deep down does it go? Is it a mere theological belief, or is it a ruling principle in your daily life? . . . what is the effect of God's mercy upon your life? God did not save you to make you happy. He saved you in order to make you serve and worship, and commune with him. Then happiness will come.'

What I do believe is this. The effects of meeting with God within our lives will be radical. Nothing will ever be the same again. The temptation to pretend that it can be will return time and again. The Devil will want us to act as though nothing has happened. His great interest is to get men and women to deny that God ever did anything. That trick is as old as man himself.

To have met with God, to have felt the touch of his Spirit in your life, to know the new sense of reality, power, joy, love and vitality that it brings is to realise at the same time that God does all that for a purpose. Isaiah discovered that when he heard the divine voice:

> 'Then I heard the voice of the Lord saying "Whom shall I send? And who will go for us?" And I said, "Here am I, send me!"' (Isaiah 6.8).

Too often we imagine that the work of the Holy Spirit is for our own gratification, that the gifts he brings are for our own benefit. It is very easy to get caught up in the 'happiness-trap'. The call to which Isaiah responded could hardly be described as happy at the superficial level. My guess is that we will completely fail to see the significance of the great movement of the Holy Spirit in our time unless we perceive that God is preparing men and women in the power of his Spirit to face his call to commitment in faith and radical discipleship for Jesus in the world.

Some points to ponder:

(a) *God can speak to you as he chooses*

I have come to believe one thing above almost everything else: that is, God wants to speak to us. He does it by many means and his purpose is to make us aware of our need of him in our lives. Don't ignore God when he speaks to you.

Some time ago I heard the remarkable story of how God spoke to one man. He was a merchant seaman who spent his life on a container ship sailing to and fro between England and Canada. One night he was sitting on deck when suddenly a strange feeling came over him. The sea was calm and the stars were shining brightly overhead, and he felt completely out of joint, as though he were totally insignificant. Perhaps it was the vastness of the sea and the magnificence of the sky, but he felt very small indeed. The experience shook him so much that when he went to bed he could not sleep. That sensation lasted until he landed at home where he went to bed and slept for the first time in days.

During the night he had a vivid dream. When he awoke in the morning the only thing he could remember was the dream. It was a strange dream because in it someone had come to his bedside and told him to get up and get dressed and go to the market hall in the town centre. There he was to ask for the bookstall. He never read books.

After breakfast, however, he decided to follow what he had seen in the dream. He went to the market hall, found the bookstall and stood there feeling a bit sheepish. That was as far as the dream took him. He was just about to turn away when the woman at the bookstall saw him and smiled. She announced to him that she had been waiting for him. A few nights before, she had been asleep in bed when she had had a dream. In the dream she had been told that the following Saturday morning a merchant seaman would come to her bookstall and she was to give him a copy of one of the Gospels in the Good News Version.

The significance of his experience in the middle of the Atlantic suddenly became clear to the seaman. Without that challenge to his self-confidence he would never have felt the need to be at the bookstall. Without going to the bookstall he might never have heard of the love of God or of the power he could put into his life. He realised that God had been trying to get into his life.

Jesus once compared the working of the Holy Spirit to the wind:

'The wind blows wherever it pleases. You hear its sound, but you cannot tell where it comes from or where it is going. So it is with everyone born of the Spirit' (John 3.8).

(b) *God can forgive you anything!*

The four Gospels are packed full of stories of 'hopeless cases'.

There was the woman whose life was in a complete shambles, who was then with her sixth man, and the man whose mind was completely deranged, who lived in rags among the tombstones. Think of the man whose sight was totally destroyed, perhaps the result of something that

22

happened at his birth. Then there was the woman whose body was racked with pain and who had spent everything she had looking for a cure. There was also the woman who had been caught in the very act of adultery. Everybody around had already condemned her to death. Take the man who was crippled in both his legs. He had not been able to walk for more than thirty-eight years! Then there was the little boy whose spirit was in the grip of something that threw him about in fits of convulsion .... and so it goes on!

These things were not put down just for the sake of a good story. John, at the end of his Gospel tells us why they are written:

'These are written that you may believe that Jesus is the Christ, the Son of God, and that by believing you may have life in his name (John 20.31).

If you feel that you are a hopeless case, then take John's Gospel and read it again. Ask God to open your eyes to understand his power in what you are reading. Then ask him to help you as he helped those others. He will!

(c) *God can call you anywhere*

Do you remember the words of Jesus on the last great day of the feast in Jerusalem? He said:

'"If a man is thirsty, let him come to me and drink. Whoever believes in me . . . streams of living water will flow from within him." By this he meant the Spirit, whom those who believed in him were later to receive' (John 7.37–39).

God's purpose in doing something *for* you is so that he might do something *through* you! To follow the call of the Holy Spirit can be the most exciting thing a person ever does but we need to know before we embark on the journey that it might also be the most costly.

2: The heart of the matter

'I pray that out of his glorious riches he may strengthen you with power through his Spirit in your inner being' (Ephesians 3.16).

It was one afternoon in June 1974. At the time I was Chaplain to one of the colleges in the University of Durham. I had been out most of the day visiting and came home mid-afternoon to find Hilda, my wife, sitting in floods of tears at our dining-room table with her Bible open in front of her. I asked her what was wrong only to find that her tears were not of sorrow but of joy. She had made a discovery that afternoon. She had found something that she had been looking for over a good number of months.

That day she had felt completely frustrated. We had recently adopted our baby son, Jonathan, and Hilda's time was taken up caring for him. A few months before I had gone away to the renewal conference for clergy of which I spoke in the first chapter, and had come back completely changed in my attitude to faith and my work of ministry. I had discovered a new power at the heart of things, but instead of making life easier within our home, it had had the reverse effect because Hilda saw something in me that she had never seen before.

Over the intervening months a feeling of distance had risen between us and a sense of frustration had developed within Hilda. In the end she was desperate and had decided on this particular day to try and discover for herself what this power was. She put the baby to bed and sat down with her Bible. For a while she scanned through every book in the New Testament, starting at the beginning of Matthew, gradually working her way through the gospels into the epistles. Then she came to Ephesians and in chapter three read the words that stand at the head of this chapter. It was as though someone had turned a neon light on in the dark. The words stood out and suddenly she realised what it was that brought power in this new way into Christian experience: it was the presence of the Holy Spirit in full measure within the life of an individual.

Hilda and I had been Christians for many years. Our own view of Christian experience did not include what is popularly known as the 'second blessing'. It seemed to us that when people became Christians they received all they were going to receive of God's Spirit. Yet there we were, having passed through a two year period of inner frustration and searching, now coming to know in a new way what the power of the Holy Spirit really meant.

The results were profound. We did not immediately speak in tongues or manifest any of the outward gifts that folk often associate with the filling of the Spirit. It was much deeper than that. It was a new awareness of God, a new experience of his love, and a new feeling of power within life and worship and in almost every compartment of our human experience. It is something that has lived ever since that time, even though there have been moments and experiences of great difficulty and sometimes disobedience.

1. The Holy Spirit in our conversion

It has always seemed to me that the unequivocal teaching of the New Testament is that a person cannot be a Christian apart from the working of the Holy Spirit. Faith is not something that we have naturally. It is a gift from God, imparted by the power of the Holy Spirit, when we turn to God.

'For it is by grace that you have been saved, through faith — and this is not from yourselves, it is the gift of God — not by works, so that no-one can boast' (Ephesians 2.8).

Paul makes it clear in his discussion on the gifts of the Spirit that the very basis of Christian experience is the confession that 'Jesus is Lord' and that this confession cannot be made by any human being apart from the help of the Holy Spirit:

'No one can say, "Jesus is Lord", except by the Holy Spirit!' (1 Corinthians 12.3).

In his introduction to the letter to the Ephesians he again lays stress on the role of the Holy Spirit in initial Christian experience:

'... having believed, you were marked in him with a seal, the promised Holy Spirit, who is a deposit guaranteeing our inheritance until the redemption of those who are God's possession' (Ephesians 1.13, 14).

John, in his Gospel, is just as clear. He recalls the occasion of the meeting between Nicodemus, the Jewish teacher, and Jesus.

'Unless a man is born of water and the Spirit, he cannot enter the kingdom of God' (John 3.5).

When we turn to God in repentance at least two important things happen. Firstly, the Spirit imparts to us that gift of faith which enables us to put our trust in God for salvation. Secondly, the Spirit puts on our hearts his imprint which tells us that we belong to God.

'The Spirit himself testifies with our spirit that we are God's children' (Romans 8.16).

'Born of water and of the Spirit'. These words describe the normal and essential state of every person who is a true believer. 'Water' refers to the reality of our human birth, generated in the womb by human conception, while 'Spirit' refers to the reality of our spiritual birth, generated in our spirits by divine conception.

2. The Spirit in our Christian living

It is clear, however, that not every Christian lives in the fullness of the Holy Spirit. It is significant that it is to the very people who are described as having been 'marked in him with a seal, the promised Holy Spirit' (Ephesians 1.13) that the prayer is addressed in Ephesians 1. 17–19. The New International Version provides us with a very clear translation of the text:

'I keep asking that the God of our Lord Jesus Christ, the glorious Father, may give you the Spirit of wisdom and revelation, *so that you know him better*'.

The passage goes on to pray that we will experience within ourselves the hope to which we have been called in Jesus and the power for living that is 'available to us who believe in God' (J. B. Phillips). These are the very things which the fullness of the Holy Spirit opens for us: an ever-increasing awareness and knowledge of God within our lives (see 2 Corinthians 3.18), an experimental grasp of all 'the wonderful blessings he promises his people' (Ephesians 1.18, TEV.) and an inward experience of the power of Jesus through the Spirit:

'That power is like the working of his mighty strength, which he exerted in Christ when he raised him from the dead and seated him at his right hand in the heavenly realms' (Ephesians 1. 19, 20).

It was the words from chapter 3.16 of the very same letter that brought such a dramatic effect within Hilda's life:

'I pray that out of his glorious riches he may strengthen you with power through his Spirit in your inner being.'

She suddenly realised that the very thing she was missing was available to her in the strength of the Holy Spirit and that God's will for her life was not to live in some kind of spiritual limbo, knowing that she was a Christian through conversion, but experiencing very little of the daily power that was meant to be at the heart of her living for Christ. It is that very contradiction of spirit that has led many of us to become aware that we need more of God and that we need his help if we are to live anything like the kind of lives he means us to. Apart from that power within us our Christian living is like a heavy load of do's and don'ts and it is very difficult to find the liberty and joy that are meant to be the hallmarks of real

Christian experience. Jesus said:

'Whoever believes in me, as the Scripture has said, streams of living water will flow from within him' (John 7.38).

One autumn, a couple of years ago, I opened my diary to discover to my delight that about three weeks ahead there were four days or so that were not booked up. I made the decision on the spot to have a break and go away for a few days.

I had always had a secret ambition to go on a canal-barge holiday and so I telephoned a well-known national firm who hired out canal boats. The lady on the other end of the phone was quite interested and asked what month we would like to go, presuming it would be the following year. I announced that I wanted to go within the next three weeks and discovered there was a surfeit of boats from which to choose at that time of year. We ended up sailing on the South Oxford canal for four days.

I learned a profound lesson on that holiday. When I arrived at the boatyard the attendant proceeded to give me the low-down on how to drive one of these boats. At the end he showed me a strange looking tool with a dog-leg bend, a handle at one end and a square-shaped hole at the other. The significance of this did not dawn on me until much later when we arrived at our first lock. Then I discovered that this was the lock-key that was used to open and close the sluices at each end of the lock. It was the experience of entering what was called an 'empty' lock that intrigued me. Of course it wasn't empty at all! There was at least enough water in it to float the boat. It just wasn't full.

We had to sail the boat into the empty lock. Then we had to close the gates behind us, guide the barge to the other end, and open up the sluice gate to let the water in. The water would rush in, lifting the boat up to a new, higher level from whence we could sail out. Without that fairly strenuous procedure there was no progress to be made on the journey up the canal.

I discovered that it is like that with our experience of God. Many of us know God to one degree or another but we are not unlike a canal boat sitting in an empty lock. It is not that there is no water there but we are just not full. We have enough experience to keep us afloat in the Christian life, but not enough to take us ahead into the higher reaches of discipleship.

I think also that this is why to be filled with the Holy Spirit cannot be described as a 'once-for-all' experience. Paul's injunction in Ephesians 5.18, rendered in most English versions: 'Be filled with the Spirit', would best be translated, 'Go on being filled with the Spirit'.

However, we all need to come at some time to that first lock. There needs to be a conscious awareness that we have come as far as we can as we are. There needs to be a closing of the doors behind us, in an inner spiritual sense, and an opening up to a fresh infilling of the water of the Holy Spirit.

In the same way that we encounter a number of locks in a canal we need to come time and again to receive fresh power and infilling from God; to go on being filled with the Spirit. There is just as much danger today amongst charismatic Christians in claiming a once-for-all experience of baptism in the Spirit as there was from evangelical Christians staking everything on that one experience of conversion years ago. Unless there is an ongoing reality of the Spirit in our lives we will lose the freshness and meaning of that past experience. What is clear is that we need to be filled. If we have never known the experience of being filled with the Spirit, then we need to. If we have known that experience then we need to go on being filled.

3. The power of the Spirit

To discover the power of the Holy Spirit in this way leads to change in a number of important areas of Christian living.

(a) *Power to live a new life*

J. B. Phillip's translation of Ephesians 1.19 has always lived for me:

'That you may know how tremendous is the power available to those of us who believe in God.'

We have all experienced something of the exasperation

29

described by Paul in Romans 7.15-24 which is caused by the tension between the desire to do what is right and good, and the reality of doing wrong. The truth about most of us is that we are a walking civil war. The only way out for Paul is the only way out for any one of us: 'Thanks be to God — through Jesus Christ our Lord' (Romans 7.25).

The same affirmation is found in the verse that came alive for Hilda in her own search:

'He may strengthen you with power through his Spirit in your inner being' (Ephesians 3.16).

(b) *Power to share Jesus with others*

This, of course, was the first effect of Pentecost. When the Spirit fell in tongues of fire on those who were waiting in the upper room, there followed the most powerful witness to the Resurrection the world has ever seen: three thousand people responded in repentance to the presence of God in the lives of these untutored men.

The change in the disciples was absolutely phenomenal. A short time before, they had been scared to show their faces in public, fearing that those who had crucified Jesus would turn their wrath on his followers and they would suffer the same fate as their Master. Now that fear had disappeared, and men who had had nothing to say and no power to say anything anyway, were out in the streets of Jerusalem witnessing boldly to the fact and significance of the resurrection of Jesus.

Indeed, Peter, who had led the retreat at the time of the crucifixion of Jesus, now stood up and pointed the finger at those who had crucified him. He did it with such effect that there was not even an attempt to produce evidence against him. Yes, the outcome of the coming of the Spirit in power was that these first Christians were given a new capability and strength to proclaim the meaning of Jesus. It has been the same ever since. True witness takes a movement and experience of the Spirit of God. Without that we are just giving lectures about facts that long ago lost their relevance to most people. When, however, in the power of his Spirit, Jesus lives again in the lives of his followers in a dynamic way, in the present tense, it has a dramatic effect on other people.

Pentecost was the first instalment of the fulfilment of the

promise that Jesus had given to his followers before he left them:

> 'You will receive power when the Holy Spirit comes on you: and you will be my witnesses in Jerusalem, and in all Judea and Samaria, and to the ends of the earth' (Acts 1.8).

I recall a very different state of affairs in my own life. When I was a teenager a few of us used to visit the neighbouring villages in our valley in south-west Scotland to engage in visitation evangelism. With great gusto we would cycle into the villages, gospel texts slung over the back wheels of our bikes, our pockets bulging with evangelistic leaflets. We went round every house in the village knocking on the doors, hoping to speak to the occupants and leave some appropriate literature. I used to knock on the door and then pray that no one would be at home, so that I could slip the tract through the letter-box and go away feeling justified that I had fulfilled my task of witnessing to Jesus.

What a difference when the Holy Spirit fills your heart and the life of Jesus bubbles within you in such a way that you cannot contain it! No longer does it depend on following a set ritual. There is a power inside you which has made Jesus real to you, and has made you want to talk about him.

For myself, as a minister of a church, it was here that I felt the first effect of being filled with the Holy Spirit. The strain of having to preach twice every Sunday had been very real. It had often been a struggle to prepare something worthwhile for the Sunday services and I well remember my feelings of panic and inadequacy, but when the Spirit came there was a new freedom. Things worked in my spirit that became creative in the lives of other people and the Word of God came alive with a new power. The result was liberation in the realm of preaching.

(c) *Power to fulfil God's purposes*

> 'For we are God's workmanship, created in Christ Jesus to do good works, which God has prepared for us to do' (Ephesians 2.10).

We do not become Christians on the strength of our goodness, but the outcome of the Holy Spirit's power in us ought to be that we are now able to fulfil those things which God means us to be involved in. We are filled with the Spirit to equip us for service in the world. Indeed, James in his letter makes these good works the very tests of our claim to be real Christians:

'Show me your faith without deeds, and I will show you my faith by what I do' (James 2.18).

The work of the Spirit within us is not just to make us feel better but to give us the strength and power to go out in the name of God and meet the needs of other people. It is this reality of faith issuing in deeds that saves us from an artificial piety that can be strangely divorced from the real world of other men and women.

Some time ago I paid a visit to the museum in Bayeux in Normandy and saw the famous tapestry that depicts the exploits of William the Conqueror and his landings at Hastings and the battle with Harold. In the tapestry is a famous scene where the mail-clad troops are marching forward into battle. Behind them is a figure who looks not unlike the rest of the soldiers, but on closer examination you can see that he is depicted as a religious figure. The inscription underneath, that explains this part of the tapestry, reads: 'Bishop Odon comforts the troops'.

What he is doing is riding behind the rest of the soldiers with a pike in his hand urging them forward into battle.

It's a bit like that with the Holy Spirit. We read in John 14.16 the promise of Jesus to his disciples that he would send them 'another Comforter' (Authorised Version). Jesus did not mean that when the Holy Spirit came he would pat us on the head and molly-coddle us all the time, but that he would stand alongside us, urging us on and giving us the help and advice that we need if we are to become God's active agents in the name of Jesus in the world at large.

(d) *Power to praise God*

I remember the morning after I had come to know the power of the Holy Spirit in that new way. It happened up in the south-east of Scotland and I had to drive all the way down through the Border country to Newcastle-upon-Tyne. I can hardly recall any of that journey because of the experience of praise in my heart. It was as though something new had been released inside me. I just wanted to sing and sing. Even years later I can recall the very words that gripped my heart that day. They were the words of a simple spiritual song:

> 'Peace is flowing like a river,
> Flowing out through you and me,
> Spreading out into the desert,
> Setting all the captives free.'

It went on and on—'Joy is flowing like a river'—'Love is flowing like a river'. It was as though the words of the Psalmist had come true for me:

> 'He put a new song in my mouth,
> a hymn of praise to our God.
> Many will see and fear
> and put their trust in the Lord' (Psalm 40.3).

It wasn't only the preaching that was so effective on the first Pentecost. It was the continual praise amongst the people as they met with joy every day and sang praise to the Lord in the temple.

The first area in which most people come to experience the gifts of the Holy Spirit is in the realm of worship. He puts a new joy for God in their hearts and he releases new gifts of worship into their lives. The gift of tongues comes alive for many people in worship. There is real liberation of spirit, something is set free inside them and deep feelings of praise rise up and come on to their lips.

> 'We worship by the Spirit of God who glory in Christ Jesus and who put no confidence in the flesh' (Philippians 3.3).

4. Resisting the Spirit

If these are some of the areas that are affected when we are filled with the Holy Spirit why are some of us so hesitant about

33

the experience? It is clear from Scripture that God does not intend there to be first and second class Christians. It is clear that he does not mean us to live our lives in continual weakness and joylessness. The invitation of Jesus is universal:

> 'So I say to you, Ask and it will be given to you; seek and you will find; knock and the door will be opened to you. For everyone who asks receives; he who seeks finds; and to him who knocks the door will be opened. .... If you then, though you are evil, know how to give good gifts to your children, how much more will your Father in heaven give the Holy Spirit to those who ask him!' (Luke 11.9, 10, 13).

There are a number of reasons why many people resist the work of the Holy Spirit.

Ignorance

It is almost as though we were in the same position as those people at Ephesus about whom we read in Acts 19. When Paul met them it soon became clear that, although they were believers to a certain extent, their understanding of what it meant to be a follower of Jesus was inadequate. They were lacking in two significant areas. Firstly, their knowledge of the Holy Spirit was deficient, and, secondly, their experience of baptism was incomplete. They had never heard of the Holy Spirit and they had not been baptised into the name of Jesus. The implication of the second statement seems to be that, although they were clear that they needed to turn away from their old life, and so had followed John the Baptist's teaching about repentance, they had never experienced the positive victory of Jesus. They had not turned to a new way of life in the power and forgiveness of Christ. The remedy lay in two directions. Firstly, they were fulfilled in their experience of baptism, and, secondly, they were ministered to in the power of the Holy Spirit (see Acts 19.56).

This was the problem in my own case. It was not, of course, that I had never heard of the Holy Spirit. It was just that the fellowship into which I had been born as a Christian sat very loose to any talk about Holy Spirit experience. It operated with an understanding of doctrine that limited the experience of Pentecost to the early days of the Church and taught that spiritual gifts had died out after the death of the last apostle and/or the closure of the canon of the New Testament scripture. The result was that I had no expectation of anything happening in my life as a direct result of being filled with the Holy Spirit.

The first step towards opening myself to the filling of the Spirit, therefore, was the enlargement of my own understanding of the work of the Holy Spirit. A blockage had to be removed from my mind. When I saw that the Holy Spirit brings new life and power, then a whole new dimension of possible experience of God was revealed to me.

Disobedience

In some cases it is the reverse of what has already been said. It is very clear to some people what the Holy Spirit wants to do in their lives, and, even more, needs to do. For that very reason they refuse to be more open to God because there are things in their lives that would need to go if the Holy Spirit were to fill them and make the Lordship of Jesus real in every part. Sometimes it is a straight choice between what they want and what they know God wants.

Fear

The words of Paul to Timothy are very pertinent for some of us:

> 'For God did not give us a spirit of timidity, but a spirit of power, of love, and of self-discipline'
> (2 Timothy 1.7).

I was met on the first night of a conference by a young man. He came up to me after the first meeting and confessed that he had been frightened to come to the conference in case, as he put it, 'I would see something in my life that needs to be sorted out.' I reassured him that he had no need to fear that. Only if God looked into his life and pinpointed something did he need to take it seriously.

The feeling he was expressing, however, is a common one with many people. The devil breeds fear. Fear is his most effective tool in the lives of a great many people. He deals in the realms of the unknown and the 'not-yet'. Many people are afraid that if they let the Holy Spirit have his way with them they will be turned into some kind of freak or their personality will undergo some radical change.

When people feel like that it is quite wrong to pretend to them that nothing changes when the Spirit comes. Often, when God works within human lives, the change is radical! What they need to be assured of is that he loves them more than anything else. Whatever he wants to do in their lives is out of his love for them.

'There is no fear in love. But perfect love drives out fear, because fear has to do with punishment. The man who fears is not made perfect in love' (1 John 4.18).

The Holy Spirit is against fear. His ministry is to remove the anxiety, worry and confusion that the Devil breeds in our hearts:

'God has poured out his love into our hearts by the Holy Spirit, whom he has given to us' (Romans 5.5).

5. How to be open to the Holy Spirit

(a) *Recognise your need of him within your life*

God's business is to create in our hearts a thirst for himself. Often the first move of the Holy Spirit within our experience is to create a feeling of dissatisfaction with how we are. We begin to be aware of a lack of power in some vital area of our life, or lack of reality within our praying or worship. It may be that God will use an extreme situation to make us aware of our total inadequacy. God doesn't play on our needs; he meets them! He is aware of them and he wants us to be aware of them so that we will come to him for the help that is needed to meet that particular need. The Holy Spirit addresses himself to the thirst in our hearts for something more. Then the invitation of Jesus becomes real to us:

'If a man is thirsty; let him come to me and drink!' (John 7.37).

(b) *Understand the promises of God to you*

The Scriptures are full of promises. Perhaps the simplest step to take is to open your Bible at Luke 11.9-13 and realise that it is a promise of the Word of God and that God wants to, and will, fulfill that promise in your own experience. He will meet you in your need. Ask God to make those promises real within your heart and receive them in faith. What God does in your life does not depend on how you feel about it but on what he has promised to do.

(c) *Be open to God filling you with the Holy Spirit*

God never forces himself on anyone, but whenever he is invited he comes into a life.

Not long ago I spoke with a man who had been trying for a number of years to find the power of God within his life. He had prayed and searched and read his Bible but nothing seemed to happen. It was so simple in the end. I asked what he did when there was a knock on his door at home. He said that he opened the door. Then what? He invited the person who was standing on the doorstep to come in. Then what? Did he carry the person into the house or did he frog-march him in? Of course not. The answer is that when the door had been opened and the invitation given, the person on the outside walked in.

It's like that with Jesus. By his Holy spirit he enters our experience.

'Here I am,' he says, 'I stand at the door and knock. If anyone hears my voice and opens the door, I will go in and eat with him, and he with me' (Revelation 3.20).

We often quote these words as though they were intended for people who were not Christians, but they are addressed to members of the Christian community at Laodicea. They are addressed to us too! We need to open ourselves and invite the Spirit of Jesus to come in – and he will. There is no formula or special mechanism. *He will come in!*

(d) *Pray*

It sometimes helps to get someone to pray with you and for

you. A simple prayer is all you need at first:

Lord Jesus, thank you for showing me how much I need you. Thank you for your promise of power through your Holy Spirit. I believe that the promise you have given is for every one who asks and that they will receive your promise for themselves. I open my life to you now and ask you to fill me with your Holy Spirit. Amen.

Live in the faith that Jesus hears your prayer and will fulfill his word in your life, for he says:

'Everyone who asks receives; he who seeks finds; and to him who knocks the door will be opened' (Luke 11.10).

3: A Matter of Priority

'Therefore, since we are receiving a kingdom that cannot be shaken, let us be thankful, and so worship God' (Hebrews 12.28).

John was a strange case. I had been asked to see him by some colleagues who had tried unsuccessfully to help him. He had been in and out of the local psychiatric unit a number of times, but to no avail. What was happening was this. John went to bed at night and locked the door of his college room behind him. In the middle of the night his fellow students were often disturbed by shouts and screams coming from John's room. When they broke into his room they would find him lying naked on the bed covered in perspiration and obviously frightened out of his mind.

There seemed no reasonable explanation of what was happening and so I was asked to see John on the off-chance that a new approach would uncover some factor that had not been taken into account.

We met each Wednesday for three weeks and by the third week I seemed to have tried every angle of approach and asked every conceivable question. I was just about to let John go when a strange thing happened. As he was rising to leave, a voice inside my head told me to ask him about his summer holiday the year before. It seemed a very strange thought but it persisted, so, in the end, I asked him where he had gone for his holiday. He told me that he had been to Cornwall with a college friend to visit an old aunt of the friend. It was nothing special but there had been one interesting feature of the holiday. It had not bothered him, but it had obviously lodged in his mind. 'She was a witch of some sort,' he said.

I became aware that we had suddenly hit on something that no one else had discussed with John. After all, it did not seem very important, and yet something had happened in that man's subconscious as a result of that meeting which had led to the havoc in his mind and the terrifying nocturnal experiences. I asked John if he would mind if I said a prayer with him. He was not a Christian and I had sat light to this for the previous three weeks, but he had no objection.

I started to pray very simply in the name of Jesus. Halfway through the prayer there was a noise and when I opened my eyes to see what was happening, John was on the floor. He had slid feet first off his chair and was lying unconscious at my feet. I really had no idea what the next step should be, but decided that, since I had started praying, I had better finish. I found myself praying into the Resurrection. It was a powerful feeling almost as though I could feel the stone being rolled away. There was another shuffle and when I looked, John was standing in front of me with eyes as clear as a bell. He shook himself like a dog coming out of sleep and asked what had happened. I explained to him as much as I knew. To my knowledge John has never suffered another bad night's sleep as a result of those awful dreams.

I learnt a whole number of important lessons through that experience which have been supported by many incidents in different ministry situations since then.

The first thing that happened was that I became aware of just how powerful are some of the forces that dominate the lives of men and women. I have come to recognise through many such experiences that the New Testament is quite right when it speaks of people being under spiritual domination:

'As for you, you were dead in your transgressions and sins, in which you used to live when you followed the ways of this world and of the ruler of the kingdom of the air, the spirit who is now at work in those who are disobedient' (Ephesians 2.1,2).

It sometimes amazes me to discover just how trivial are the things to which we give authority within our lives. Even seemingly harmless things like food and drink and the hobbies we enjoy are allowed to take over our lives to such a degree that everything else is pushed out to the fringe. In other cases it is the darker and more sinister and secret things of the mind and spirit that dominate the whole of life. Again and again the truth is demonstrated that we are not free agents. Every one of us seems to be in chains to one thing or another.

The second thing I learned that day was about the authority of Jesus in such situations. I had read many times in the Gospels about the kingdom of God but not until that moment had its real significance come sharply home to me. At the beginning of his ministry Jesus proclaimed:

'Repent, for the kingdom of heaven is near' (Matthew 4.17).

The four Gospels throb with teaching about the kingdom of God. I recommend that you take time to read Howard Snyder's *The Community of the King*. At one point he says this:

'Jesus' mission was to tell the good news of the kingdom, show what the kingdom was like, demonstrate its works, tell how to enter it, and establish the messianic community in embryonic form. He died on the Cross and rose again to defeat the kingdom of evil and bring in the age of the kingdom of God.'

The Gospels proclaim that in Jesus something new has arrived. It is not that God has not been at work before, but here, in the life of this one man, God's authority is expressed to a new degree. Never had the rule of God been more clearly demonstrated in terms of a human life. Even a Roman centurion, who himself lived and worked under authority, recognised that in Jesus he was dealing with someone who acted in the name of an even higher authority (see Matthew 8:9). The secret of Jesus' power did not lie in his charismatic personality or in a rare gift of communication. It lay in the fact that his life was completely open to the power of God. It was lived as an expression of the kingdom of God and his power came from that source.

At times that authority mystified people, at other times it infuriated them. With one breath they asked the question, 'Isn't this the carpenter's son?' With the next they were demanding, 'Where does he get the right to do such things?' Matthew's Gospel, in particular, echoes with the sounds of the kingdom of God. The power of the kingdom was shown by the fact that Jesus cast out demons in the power of God's Spirit. The antidote, as far as Jesus was concerned, to all the forces of spiritual evil that held men and women in their grip, was the reality of the power of the rule of God within their lives.

'If I drive out demons by the Spirit of God, then the kingdom of God has come upon you' (Matthew 12.28).

The presence and principles of the kingdom of God were disclosed in the experience of Jesus. It was the promise of Jesus that his followers, too, would, by the power of the Holy Spirit, be able to enter in to the reality of the kingdom.

'The knowledge of the secrets of the kingdom of heaven has been given to you, but not to them' (Matthew 13.11).

The Church today has been given the awesome but exciting task of proclaiming the reality of this power and authority of God in the lives of men and women all over the world:

'This gospel of the kingdom will be preached in the whole world as a testimony to all nations, and then the end will come' (Matthew 24.14).

The exciting thing about proclaiming the kingdom is that it is not only the repetition of a story. It is not just the utterance of a few hopeful thoughts about what we might expect God to do, but it is the explanation of what God is already doing! This was the hallmark of the preaching of Peter at Pentecost: he explained the events of God that had taken place right in their midst.

'Let all Israel be assured of this: God has made this Jesus, whom you crucified, both Lord and Christ' (Acts 2.36).

The result of that declaration was that three thousand or so people responded to the call of the kingdom. The challenge of the kingdom of God is the challenge of *event*. It is demonstrable. It can be seen and, better still, it can be experienced. In the words of Paul:

'The kingdom of God is not a matter of talk but of power' (1 Corinthians 4.20).

This is what makes people sit up and take notice: not the preaching of yet another sermon of dubious relevance, but evidence, in terms that they can understand, that God is at work doing something real within our lives. Anybody can talk, and, indeed, false spiritual movements are often characterised by complicated and long-winded statements about belief. It takes a power above normal, however, to achieve the healing and sorting out that is needed with the twisted and knotty experience that is the real world for many folks today. It is no accident that Jesus pointed out the very same thing to John the Baptist when John sent some of his followers to enquire about the authenticity of the work of Jesus:

'Go back and report to John what you hear and see: the blind receive sight, the lame walk, those who have leprosy are cured, the deaf hear, the dead are raised, and the good news is preached to the poor' (Matthew 11.4,5).

In John's experience, of which I spoke at the start of this chapter, I suddenly became aware of the power of the name of Jesus. I discovered, almost by accident, that it was possible to pray with someone and to expect God to break into their lives with all the power of his kingdom. The reasons are now clear to me, of course. John was in the grip of the power of another kingdom. The New Testament describes that as 'the kingdom of darkness'. It needed a stronger power to enter John's life to free him from its grip.

It causes me great sadness when I reflect on how much ignorance and unbelief there is today among clergy and church leaders about this whole area of human experiences. Fear of the extreme and the weird has shut us off, in the main, from the fact that a great number of people around us live every day under the power of very profound forces of spiritual evil. I can honestly say that not one part of all my theological and pastoral training prepared me in any way for encounter with this fact. Because they live in ignorance of the dynamic reality of the kingdom of God many people pass through their lives never freed from powers from which only the authority of Jesus can liberate them.

The truth of the kingdom of God is not offered to the Church as something to be discussed and theorised about, but as something to be lived in! The arrival of the kingdom has a number of important repercussions for our lives.

1. The presence of the kingdom

The great cry of Jesus is summed up in the words of Luke 17.21:

'The kingdom of God is within you'.

Jesus had something to say and many were confounded by the power of his words, but ultimately it was what he did that challenged them. Things happened wherever he went. This, for me, is the great benefit that has come from our experience of the Holy Spirit in our own day. It is the fact that God still does things. If we didn't have this evidence, we might be forgiven for suspecting that he did not really exist. However, when there is unmistakable evidence of the power of the Holy Spirit in people's living, it is far more difficult to gainsay the fact of his existence.

The fact that the kingdom of God has come is significant in a number of ways:

(a) *It means that a new authority has entered the realm of my human experience*

That was the call of Jesus at the outset of his own ministry: 'Repent, for the kingdom of heaven is near' (Matthew 4.17). Jesus was challenging men to turn away (for that is what repentance really means) from all the things that were dominating them and to find through him a new power from God that would lead to freedom.

The student, John, had not been free. Something had gripped his spirit and it took the entrance of the authority of

God in the Spirit of Jesus to liberate him. We all need to experience this liberating authority.

Ultimately, the Christian gospel is not a set of propositions. It is not a philosophy of life offered as an alternative to the many philosophies that already vie for a place in our minds. It is a power! It is a power that is greater than any other power! It is the power of God himself coming into my life and taking authority over everything else that dominates me. Jesus made that very claim:

'How can anyone enter a strong man's house and carry off his possessions unless he first ties up the strong man?' (Matthew 12.29). *out of context*

Jesus recognised the fact that people are in the grip of some pretty powerful forces in their daily lives and that it takes all the authority of God to break that power. John, in his letter at the end of our New Testament underlines the same point:

'You . . . are from God and have overcome them,
because the one who is in you is greater than the one
who is in the world' (1 John 4.4).

In the life of Jesus we see the coming of the kingdom with authority. He has shown us that there is no power on earth that he cannot overcome. The word in the Gospels for this authority in which Jesus acted is a very interesting word. It is the Greek word *exousia*. It occurs time and again in the Gospels in relation to Jesus. An even more interesting fact is that it is the very same word that is used in John's Gospel to describe the secret of the new life that Jesus brings to those who believe in him:

'To all who received him, to those who believed in his name, he gave the right (*exousia*) to become children of God' (John 1.12).

To live as a child of God is to live with all the authority and power of the kingdom of God at the heart of our experience!

To speak of Jesus as King is not to imagine him literally with a golden crown living in the style of an earthly monarch. It is something much more profound than that. In the day when Jesus proclaimed his kingship, Caesar Augustus ruled supreme throughout the Roman Empire. It seemed as though nothing in the world was outside his control and influence, but Jesus recognised that there were many other sources of authority within the lives of men and women that had nothing to do with the political and secular power of Rome. So he proclaimed that his kingdom was not of this world. He did not mean that what he was saying was irrelevant to the here and now, but he meant that he was dealing with areas of authority that *were* the real world in which men and women participated.

He also drew his authority from a higher source than Caesar and it is an authority that stands in direct opposition to those hidden powers that seek to dominate the hearts of men. The ultimate evidence of this power of God, as far as the New Testament is concerned, is shown in the fact that God raised Jesus from the dead 'far above all rule and authority, power and dominion, and every title that can be given, not only in the present age, but also in the one to come' (Ephesians 1.21).

The practical result of this for us is spelled out by Paul in Ephesians 1.18–20. J. B. Phillips gives a most stimulating rendering of it:

'That you may realise how tremendous is the power *available* to us who believe in God. That power is the same divine energy which was demonstrated in Christ when he raised him from the dead ...'

This means that all the authority of God's kingdom is available in the present tense of our own lives. That is why, when I prayed with John, it felt as though the Resurrection was taking place at that moment. In a real sense it was! Just as God through his Spirit had rolled the stone away from the tomb in which Jesus lay and liberated him into new life, so he was breathing new life into John and rolling away the great stone of fear and doubt that had held him in bondage. This is what Jesus said had been hidden from the 'wise and learned' and had been revealed to little children.

'All things have been committed to me by my Father. No one knows the Son except the Father, and no one knows the Father except the Son and those to whom the Son chooses to reveal him' (Matthew 11.27).

(b) *It means that we can act in this authority as we touch the lives of other people*

One of the first results of the experience of the Holy Spirit at Pentecost was that the disciples were able to act in this authority of the kingdom. It was not their own and it could not be imitated, as later events were to prove, but as Peter and John went up to the temple to pray they became aware of this new authority of the kingdom within them. They had no money to give the man who asked for alms, but they gave him something that he did not expect! In the words of Peter:

'Silver or gold I do not have, but what I have I give you. In the name of Jesus Christ of Nazareth, walk' (Acts 3.6).

The authority of the kingdom had arrived in that lame man's life and the first thing it did was give him a new set of legs!

(c) *It means that we can address the powers of evil in the authority of Jesus*

Time and again Jesus addressed the real power that was overpowering the human spirit. There was a directness of approach with him that would leave most of us today feeling very uncomfortable. We have managed to domesticate the power of the kingdom so that it has become something at second remove. Jesus, however, took the forces of evil head-on. Who can doubt that in our world today, for all its technical advances and scientific achievements, men and women are still in the grip of powerful and unseen forces that seek to wreck their lives?

We have seen time and again that evil is allergic to the voice of Jesus, but Jesus' authority cannot be manufactured or imitated at the human level. An incident in the experience of the early church shows this very clearly. Some travelling Jewish exorcists were trying to imitate the power of Paul to make a quick buck, but the evil spirits knew that the whole thing was unreal:

47

'The evil spirit answered them, "Jesus I know and Paul I know about, but who are you?"' (Acts 19.15).

The arrival of the kingdom means that a new authority has entered the realm of human experience. In the words of Charles Wesley:

> 'Jesus the name high over all,
> In hell or earth, or sky:
> Angels and men before it fall,
> And devils fear and fly.'

2. The priorities of the kingdom

It's a funny thing, but I was brought up to believe that all this talk of the kingdom of God was something that was for the future. I was taught that it did not apply to this present moment of Christian experience, but would all become real one day when Jesus would appear in the fullness of his kingdom. Of course, the New Testament's teaching about the kingdom does have a powerful future dimension but it is certainly not limited to the future.

The passage of Scripture that always seemed to contradict a futuristic understanding of the kingdom of God is the one that contains the well known words of Jesus:

> 'Seek first his kingdom and his righteousness, and all these things will be given to you as well' (Matthew 6.33).

This speaks about priorities! It challenges us, as Christians, about where our priorities really lie. Are we, like the rest of men, caught up in a rat race of achievement and the collection of possessions, filling our lives with things that last only as long as the next fashion and which, in any event, we cannot take with us when we leave?

Nothing can be so dramatic in a world of twisted values and failed ambitions as the witness of Christians to the values that Jesus brings in the kingdom. This does not mean that Christians place no value on money or possessions or the marvellous achievements of modern technology for the benefit of the human race. It means that they put all these things in their proper place as servants of man rather than masters. These are not things to be worshipped but to be used.

God has never been slow to provide for the material as well as the spiritual needs of those who trust him, but he does it so that we are able to serve the needs of others! The great biblical image of the life of the people of God is that of pilgrimage. We are on a route-march through life with our eyes fixed on an eternal goal. 'Our citizenship is in heaven' (Philippians 3.20).

Pilgrimage is based on a very simple principle: you take as much as you need for the journey; what you have is to enable you to achieve your goal. Anything else is an extra and an encumbrance.

Three words sum up this principle in detail – simplicity, sufficiency, and sharing.

The first aspect is underlined by the writer to Hebrews:

'Keep your lives free from the love of money and be content with what you have, because God has said, "Never will I leave you, never will I forsake you"' (Hebrews 13.5).

'Godliness with contentment is great gain', said Paul to Timothy (1 Timothy 6.6). He is actually saying something that is revolutionary in a world where the whole of life revolves round the principle of discontent. The wheel of commercial viability is kept turning by the appeal to people's minds for yet another new model!

The second aspect is demonstrated in the story of the provision of the manna in the wilderness, of which we read in Exodus 16. Each person gathered according to his need. The manna was provided one day at a time, except on the day before the Sabbath, when enough was also provided to cover the day of rest that God had stipulated for the lives of his people.

'When they measured it ... he who gathered much did not have too much and he who gathered little did not have too little. Each one gathered as much as he needed' (Exodus 16.18).

It takes very little effort for us to see, in our world of expanding numbers of people and limited resources, just how radical this principle really is. Instead of living for Number One and in greed, the kingdom presents us with a challenge about the stewardship of the resources that God has provided for us to do his will.

That same story also illustrates the third aspect of the principle of kingdom life. It was the very thing that was at the heart of the witness of the early believers immediately after Pentecost.

'All the believers were one in heart and mind. No one claimed that any of his possessions were his own, but they shared everything they had ... There were no needy persons among them' (Acts 4:32, 34).

Ronald Sider in his book on radical Christian living makes the same point:

'Redeemed economic relationships in the early church resulted in an increase of the word of God. What a sobering thought! Is it perhaps the same today? Would similar economic changes produce a dramatic increase of believers today? Probably so. Are those who talk most glibly about the importance of evangelism prepared to pay that price?'

The more seriously we take this subject of the kingdom of God, the more we can see that it affects every important area of human life in a very deep way.

3. The principles of the kingdom

The principles upon which the kingdom of God rests are simply devastating! They are the complete denial of all power and aggression. The way Jesus achieves his power is in complete contradiction to the way power is achieved by a human dictator or overlord. Jesus reigns through love and the most effective instrument of his kingdom is the application of the love of God into the human heart.

A look at some of the principles we find at work in the experience of Jesus will convince us that if we are to follow the way of the kingdom then many things will need to change in our own lives.

Humiliation. I suppose we could use the word 'humility', but surely the experience of Jesus goes much deeper than that. All that we mean by humility is overshadowed by the reality of what it meant for him. To achieve the kingdom and introduce it into the hearts of men, he underwent the most profound humiliation at their hands. His victory was not achieved the easy way. His power was not that of magic. There was no wand to wave that would bring about his purposes. For him the way of power was the way of defeat and ignominy. This seems a conundrum to us, but it is the way of the kingdom. God defeats evil because he refuses to meet it on its own ground. The way of evil is the way of arrogance and aggression. God stoops to conquer! The words of Paul in Philippians chapter 2 take on a new meaning when we see them in this context:

'Your attitude should be the same as that of Christ
Jesus:
Who, being in very nature God, did not consider
equality with God something to be grasped, but made
himself nothing, taking the very nature of a servant,
being made in human likeness. And being found in
appearance as a man, he humbled himself and became
obedient to death – even death on a cross! Therefore
God exalted him to the highest place and gave him the
name that is above every name, that at the name of
Jesus every knee should bow, in heaven and on earth
and under the earth, and every tongue confess that
Jesus Christ is Lord, to the glory of God the Father'
(Philippians 2.5–11).

It goes against the grain of our human pride to suggest that this is what needs to happen in our own experience if we want to know the power of the kingdom. Yet it is true that God can only work in his power in and through the lives of those men and women in whose hearts every trace of self-aggrandisement has been put to death.

Renunciation. The words of Paul in 2 Corinthians 8.9 underline for us the second principle of the kingdom:

'For you know the grace of our Lord Jesus Christ, that
though he was rich, yet for your sakes he became poor,

so that you through his poverty might become rich.'

The words of Jesus seem at times appallingly black and white – if only we could modify them slightly – but the demand of the kingdom is total. It demands that there be nothing else in our lives to control our affections or divert our interest.

'Any of you who does not give up everything that he has cannot be my disciple' (Luke 14.33).

There is no use in trying to pretend that these are easy words for us. They were not easy words for Jesus. The victory of Calvary cost him the blood-sweat of Gethsemane. He was aware of the awful cost of allowing the power of the kingdom to work through him. It was to cost him everything he knew in terms of life and relationship.

Some of my best friends in the Christian life have found that same cost. To follow the way of Jesus has been for them very dear in terms of the things they have had to leave behind. Yet, if they had stayed with those things or relationships, in the end, those and not the kingdom of God, would have held sway within their living.

The only consolation is that this is never the end of the matter. After Gethsemane and Calvary came the glory of the Resurrection. We need to be assured in the power of the Holy Spirit that nothing is ever wasted in the kingdom of God. No sacrifice is meaningless. Jesus pointed that out:

'I tell you the truth, unless an ear of wheat falls to the ground and dies, it remains only a single seed. But if it dies, it produces many seeds' (John 12.24).

Each one of the Gospel writers homes in on the same truth. Mark puts it like this:

'No one who has left home or brothers or sisters or mother or father or children or fields for me or the gospel will fail to receive a hundred times as much in this present age ... and in the age to come, eternal life' (Mark 10.29, 30).

That is not an excuse for a 'get rich quick' mentality in spiritual things. Rather, it is the promise of the kingdom to those who will follow the way of the King. Nothing that is given away to God is wasted and the outcome of single-mindedness in God's way is always fruitfulness.

Dedication. A third important principle of the kingdom of God is portrayed for us in that remarkable verse in Luke's Gospel that describes the attitude of Jesus to what was ahead of him:

'As the time approached for him to be taken up to heaven, Jesus resolutely set out for Jerusalem' (Luke 9.51).

The older translations make it sound very determined: 'He set his face to go to Jerusalem'. For Jesus there was no turning back! Maybe one of the main reasons we don't experience the power of the kingdom is because we don't share in the tenacity of the kingdom. Too much of our religion depends on how we feel. We live at the level of our emotions and our obedience to the way of Jesus depends on whether we feel inclined to go that way. The way of the Spirit is the way of obedience. Sometimes we sing with great gusto:

'I have decided to follow Jesus,
No turning back, no turning back.
The world behind me, the Cross before me,
No turning back, no turning back.'

Other tough words from Jesus put the whole thing into perspective:

'No one who puts his hand to the plough and looks back is fit for service in the kingdom of God' (Luke 9.62).

Frankly, there are many times when I feel tempted to follow something other than the kingdom. We all have those things in our lives that make their appeal in powerful terms. In the end, however, it comes down to a straight choice. Will I follow the kingdom and be open for God to work through me or will I choose the other way, only to discover its limitations and transience?

53

At times it is a costly thing to go God's way, but there is nothing in the world worth having that is not worth paying for! I don't mean that there is the slightest chance of our earning our right to the kingdom of God by what we give up, but single-mindedness in the work of God will mean, of necessity, that there are things that other people seem free to follow that we will have to leave behind.

4. The promise of the kingdom

We live in a world of unfulfilled ambitions, unrealised dreams, and unobtainable aspirations. The result in the lives of many people has been disillusion and despair. It is little wonder that the message of the kingdom of God sounds like good news in a world like this! The gospel is a message of *promise*:

> 'The promise is for you and your children and for all who are far off – for all whom the Lord our God will call' (Acts 2.39).

Jesus wants to make the promise of his kingdom real within our experience by the power of the Holy Spirit.

(a) *It is a promise of power*

First, it is power in us. 'The kingdom of God is within you' said Jesus (Luke 7.21). That is precisely where it needs to be! We need to know within the deep reaches of our beings the power that will give us the victory over those forces that control us on the inside. The New Testament is totally realistic about the struggle of which we are all too well aware:

> 'I pray that out of his glorious riches he may strengthen you with power through his Spirit in your inner being' (Ephesians 3.16).

Second, it is power through us. The way in which Jesus speaks of his power at work within his followers makes that clear time and again. The reality of the kingdom is to be in our lives so that it can go out through our lives to others.

Jesus said: 'I tell you the truth, anyone who has faith in me will do what I have been doing. He will do even greater things than these, because I am going to the Father' (John 14.12).

It is an amazing fact that God's purpose through our lives is to continue the working of the same power that was in Jesus' life!

(b) *It is a promise of hope*

'Hope' is God's great four-letter word! He is described as 'the God of hope'. It is to share in his hope that we are born in the power of the Holy Spirit. Christian hope is not the result of watching 'News at Ten', but is the outcome of the work of the Holy Spirit as he brings us into living relationship with the God of hope.

'In his great mercy he has given us new birth into a living hope through the resurrection of Jesus Christ from the dead, and into an inheritance that can never perish, spoil or fade – kept in heaven for you' (1 Peter 1.3,4).

Hope in this sense is not a pie in the sky thing. It fixes our eyes on another world, but in so doing releases us from being over anxious in the here and now and so sets us free to be available to God and other people in their need.

This hope was present right from the start of Jesus' life. When his birth was foretold to Mary, the promise of the messenger of God made that clear:

'He will reign over the house of Jacob for ever: his kingdom will never end' (Luke 1.33).

It has been ratified for us in the resurrection of Jesus from the dead. He has broken through the confines of our mortality and proclaimed his power from the other side of the grave. He speaks with the authority of the kingdom when he says:

'I am the resurrection and the life. He who believes in me will live, even though he dies: and whoever lives and believes in me will never die' (John 11.25,26).

When the space-probe 'Voyager I' was going past Saturn, I was leading a mission within the University of Aston. As I rose to speak to the crowd, someone put a copy of the day's newspaper into my hand. The headlines proclaimed the amazing discoveries that had resulted from the voyage of the probe. It seemed that man's horizons had been widened considerably and some of his previous theories in the realm of physics were in danger of being radically revised. At the very least our knowledge of the rings of the planet Saturn was greatly increased. It is something like that with Jesus. He is the only one who has broken through the boundaries of death. He speaks with the authority of the kingdom of God when he addresses us about life here and now and there and then.

Stephen Travis, in his book *The Jesus Hope*, contrasts the hope of the kingdom of God with the gloom of all our secular twentieth century prophets.

'Most twentieth century prophets are prophets of doom, not hope – we need think only of George Orwell's *1984*, Aldous Huxley's *A Brave New World*, Anthony Burgess's *A Clockwork Orange*, Neville Shute's *On The Beach*'.

(c) *It is a promise of resources*

I have spoken elsewhere in this book of the ways in which God promises to meet all our needs. That promise extends into every area of our experience – the material, the physical and the spiritual. Paul sums up the promise of the kingdom for us when he says:

'My God will meet all your needs according to his glorious riches in Christ Jesus' (Philippians 4.19).

Some time ago when I was driving through South Devon I came across a traffic hold-up on the outskirts of one of the towns. It transpired that the main street was being repaired and traffic was being diverted a roundabout way. The large sign that caught my eye was a warning. It read: 'Beware! Changed priorities ahead!'

That is the word of the kingdom of God. It brings a whole new authority within the realm of my human experiences, it presents me with a completely new set of priorities, and it fills my life with all the promises of God.

'Seek first his kingdom and his righteousness and all these things will be given to you as well' (Matthew 6.33).

Before you read any further use this section as a spiritual check-list. Have a look in the following areas:

(a) *Awareness:*

How much am I aware of the Lordship of Christ within my experience? Does being a Christian mean that I know the reality of God's kingdom in my life?

(b) *Authority:*

What is it that rules to the greatest extent in my life? What governs my actions, attitudes and outlook? Is there anything which has an unhealthy hold over me?

(c)*Attitudes:*

What is my attitude to my possessions and material things? Do I look upon them as tools to be used for God and other people?

(d) *Ambition:*

What governs my ambitions and goals? Am I self-centred or do God's will and the needs of other people take precedence over my own wishes?

4: Preparing The Way

> *'The Spirit helps us in our weakness. We do not know what we ought to pray, but the Spirit himself intercedes for us with groans that words cannot express'* (Romans 8:26).

Prayer stands at the centre of everything else in our Christian experience. That stands to reason, for prayer is the means of our communication with God. When God becomes real through the work of his Spirit in our lives then it follows that we will feel the need to speak with him.

There is no part of my own life where the change has been more radical. Previously prayer was something I did. I saw it as a very necessary part of the discipline of my Christian life, but basically it bored me! Now it means something very different. It is how I talk to my Father. I think it is Michael Green who somewhere has described prayer as 'the Christian's two-way telephone with God'. It is the way in which faith is built up: it is through the exercise of waiting before the Lord that he communicates his vision and creates faith in our hearts. That is the reason why the Devil wants to break the chain of our prayer life. He knows that when we are out of touch with headquarters, we soon lose our way and we are at the mercy of many other voices and impulses. Prayer is the means by which I come to know the will of God. It becomes the eyesight of the Christian as well as his hearing-aid.

Prayer is of vital necessity to every part of our Christian life:

– *It is the secret of spiritual growth*. Through prayer our relationship with the Father matures and develops. As we live with him, we come to know him and the ways in which he works. Through prayer our relationship with each other matures and develops. People cannot spend time open before God and remain closed to one another. Perhaps one of the reasons we spend so little time with each other in real, waiting prayer is because we know that in that exercise there is a great risk of our inner hearts being exposed with others before the presence of God. Rather than run the risk of that we tend to withdraw.

– *It is the secret of spiritual ministry.* It is interesting to notice in Ephesians chapter 6 that Paul brings his excursus on spiritual warfare to a conclusion with the exhortation:

'Pray in the Spirit on all occasions with all kinds of prayers and requests' (Ephesians 6.18).

When he speaks in 1 Corinthians chapter 1 of the power of the Cross, Paul emphasises the 'foolishness of what we preach'. It is by that seemingly futile means that God has chosen to sow his word into the hearts of men and women to produce salvation in their lives. It is much the same with prayer. Many times when I am standing ministering to someone in prayer the Devil seeks to undermine faith by pointing out the utter foolishness of this exercise. Imagine thinking that speaking a few words over someone with a very profound need is going to do any good!

Yet time and time again the Father confounds Satan. We might almost say: 'It has pleased God through the foolishness of what we pray to save some!'

– *It is the secret of spiritual warfare.* This is a subject that warrants further consideration. Suffice it to say now that it is through prayer that we take on the powers of evil. It is here more than anywhere that the words of Romans 8.26 come true. Here we need both the Spirit's guidance on what to pray about and the Spirit's enabling on how to pray. In the arena of spiritual warfare, prayer is God's number one provision for the Christian. Someone said to me a while ago that the Bible may be the sword of the Spirit, but prayer is the Christian's inter-continental ballistic missile!

S. D. Gordon, himself a great man of prayer, highlights the power of prayer in this respect:

'Prayer is insisting upon Jesus' victory, and the retreat of the enemy on each particular spot. The enemy yields only what he must. He yields only what is taken. Therefore ground must be taken step by step. Prayer must be definite.'

1. The perspective of prayer

The perspective against which prayer operates is gained by looking in three directions:

(a) *God*

Prayer starts with our experience of God. What we think of God will ultimately be determined by how we have come to know him. If God is not real at the heart of our experience, then naturally what we look for within the exercise of our prayer life will be greatly diminished.

The older translation of Hebrews 11.6 brings the whole question into the right perspective:

'He that cometh to God must believe that he is and that he is a rewarder of them that diligently seek him' (Authorised Version).

Almost every modern translation substitutes the phrase 'he exists' for the words 'he is' of the older version. Of course, in linguistic terms the two renderings mean the same thing. To say that 'God is' is to say, at one level, that 'God exists', but at the level of the Spirit there are light years between the two translations. Millions of people believe in the existence of God but that does not mean that he is a living, personal force within their lives.

To say that 'God is' means that he is actively and dynamically present in the power of his Holy Spirit and that he can do things within the arena of human experience.

This is a major divide within the traditional Church today. There are many who want to pay lip-service to a traditional belief in God but when that belief is examined it is nothing short of a deist view of things. The deist believes that God created the universe but, now that it is set in motion, he has left the system to run itself. The question that prayer confronts is whether we believe that today God does act purposefully and creatively within the world and in the lives of men and women.

This 'God-perspective' on prayer was, of course, provided by Jesus himself. When his disciples asked him to teach them to pray, he started in the way that is familiar to us all:

'This is how you should pray:
Our Father in heaven,
hallowed be your name' (Matthew 6.9).

The words of Jesus stress the intimacy of God with his children – 'Our Father' – but they take us beyond that. I have a little boy and he frequently asks me to do things for him or give things to him. Sometimes I can, but fairly often I can't. I have all the intimacy of fatherhood but at times fall drastically short of capability. The words of E. M. Bounds remind us of just what it means to live with this God-perspective in our prayer life:

'Prayer can do *anything* God can do.'

(b) *Faith*

Faith is the key that unlocks the power of prayer. It is the eyesight of the Holy Spirit. Faith prevents us from moving and acting at the level of the merely human. Faith looks beyond the obvious into the hidden realm of the possibilities of God.

'Faith is being sure of what we hope for and certain of what we do not see' (Hebrews 11.1).

This does not mean that we live at the level of unfounded optimism or wishful thinking. Men of faith have their feet planted very squarely on the ground but it is not the same ground as others who choose not to live by faith!

This faith is itself a gift from God

We are given the power to trust God in our prayer life on the same grounds we were given to trust him for our salvation.

'For it is by grace that you have been saved, through
faith – and this is not from yourselves, *it is the gift of
God* – not by works, so that no one can boast'
(Ephesians 2.8).

*This faith is directed towards what God has already done for us in
Jesus*

Paul spells out the reality of that in Romans 8.31, 32:

'If God is for us, who can be against us? He who did
not spare his own son, but gave him up for us all – how
will he not also, along with him, graciously give us all
things?'

Faith does not act in ignorance. It may work in the dark at
times, not knowing what the next step is or where the next
provision is coming from, but in ignorance it does not work. It
has its eyes focussed clearly on the greatness of God's love as
he has shown it by giving the gift of Jesus. Surely every other
gift is only a footnote in comparison with that!

'No good thing does he withhold
from those whose walk is blameless.
O Lord Almighty,
blessed is the man who trusts in you' (Psalm 84.11).

Faith knows the measure of God's love and it takes that as the
ground for all its trust in Him.
So we can see that the way God makes prayer effective in our
lives is by planting in us the very gifts that are needed to make it
effective.

'have faith in God ... I tell you, whatever you ask for in
prayer, believe that you have received it, and it will be
yours! (Mark 11:22, 24).

(c) *The whole world*

One exciting outcome of seeing that prayer is a two-way
exercise between myself and God is that I am immediately
introduced to the fact that I can be brought into touch with any
part of God's kingdom through prayer. As I am open in spirit
before Him He may lay situations on my mind and heart that

are far outside the boundaries of my own experience.

Prayer encompasses the whole globe. Some words from S.D. Gordon witness to the fact that men of prayer like him from years ago experienced the very same truth:

'Prayer puts one in touch with a planet. I can as really be touching hearts for Him in far away India or China through prayer as though I were there . . . a man may go outside today, and shut his door, and as really spend half an hour in India for God as though he were there in person.'

We would have less difficulty in wondering what we might pray about if we realised that if we waited with open hearts and minds before God he would print things there that go far beyond our imagination.

I heard a recent account of how that worked in relation to a group of Christians who were waiting in prayer one night in the south of England. During their prayer time a number of them had a strong impression that they should pray for the Anglican Bishop in Teheran. The feeling was very strong and persisted in such a way that they began to bear the bishop up in prayer before the Lord though they had no idea why there were doing this.

To their amazement, not long afterwards they discovered just why they had had that strong impression. At that very time when the believers were praying in England a drama was taking place in the home of the bishop. He was asleep in bed with his wife when a number of armed men broke into the room and fired some shots at him from close range. Every one of those shots missed their target and went into the pillow. The only injury that was sustained was to the bishop's wife who had thrown herself over her husband to protect him. That night God used the open hearts of those English believers to build a wall of protecting faith round the bishop.

2. The dynamics of prayer

One of the chief reasons for the feeling of dullness in our prayer lives is the fact that so often prayer is looked upon as a human operation. We tend to think that it all depends on us. Romans 8.26 gives the lie to that:

'We do not know what we ought to pray' (or, as the alternative translations reads, 'how to pray'), 'but the Spirit himself intercedes for us with groans that words cannot express.'

The module printed below demonstrates how, at every point in the exercise of prayer, it is the Holy Spirit who takes the initiative. This helps us to know what to expect when we wait with open hearts before the presence of God. We know now that we are not merely coming to present our shopping lists or to fulfil a daily obligation. What we are actually doing when we pray is being still before God and making our minds and hearts available to him that he might operate within them in the power of his Spirit.

When we do that, the Spirit begins to lead us into deep realms of understanding – both of ourselves and of the purpose of God.

The Spirit's dynamics in prayer

Divine initiative		Human response		Faith-effect
Conviction	→	Confession	→	Cleansing
Recollection	→	Thanksgiving	→	Praise
Motivation	→	Intercession	→	Understanding
Communication	→	Assurance	→	Action

The words on the left represent the movements of the Spirit within our hearts as he begins to work in us. The words in the middle column represent the effect of the work of the Holy Spirit in our own spirits. The words in the right hand column represent the outcome of the Spirit's work in and through us, as we are taken from one level of faith at work to the next.

(a) *Conviction*

The first work of the Holy Spirit within human experience is always conviction. He makes us aware of our failure and shortcomings in the presence of God. He gets under our skin and makes us feel uncomfortable about those things within our lives that prevent the power of God working through us.

Jesus himself pointed out this primary work of the Spirit:

'When he comes, he will convict the world of guilt in
regard to sin and righteousness and judgment'
(John 16.8).

It does not matter at what stage of Christian experience we
might find ourselves: we always need the ongoing work of the
Spirit in conviction. God shines his light through our hearts
and exposes those dark areas where unbelief and doubt lurk.
One of the chief reasons we don't like to take time with God
alone in quiet is because we have learned from experience that
when we do he begins to speak to us about ourselves and to
highlight those things in our lives with which he needs to deal.

'If we claim to be without sin, we deceive ourselves and
the truth is not in us. If we confess our sins, he is
faithful and just and will forgive us our sins and purify
us from all unrighteousness' (1 John 1.8).

The Psalmist posed the question:

'Who may ascend the hill of the Lord?
Who may stand in his holy place?' (Psalm 24.3).

The answer is uncomfortably plain. No human being in the
world can qualify to enter God's presence in prayer without
first having forgiveness through Jesus.

'He who has clean hands and a pure heart,
who does not lift up his soul to an idol
or swear by what is false' (Psalm 24.3, 4).

The language may belong to another age but the truth that
lies at its heart is absolutely for today. Prayer is a relationship
and, as with any other deep relationship, it can only operate
when heart is open with heart and the way of deep personal
communication is clear. A true exercise of prayer in the Holy
Spirit starts with the Holy Spirit clearing the way within us
for God.

Conviction leads to confession and confession leads to
cleansing, for,

'The blood of Jesus, his Son, purifies us from every sin' (1 John 1.7).

(b) *Recollection*

The thing, above all, that is going to bring power into our prayer life is the recollection of all that God has done for us. We need to start with the massive things. So often we thank God for the trivialities, but the thing that gives greatest pleasure to the heart of God is when we are able to recount all the blessings of his work for us through Jesus. That is at the centre of his interest.

'Through Jesus, therefore, let us continually offer to God a sacrifice of praise – the fruit of lips that confess his name' (Hebrews 13.15).

It is the work of the Holy Spirit within us to bring to mind the importance of Jesus:

'He will bring glory to me by taking from what is mine and making it known to you' (John 16.14).

That is one of those texts with many hidden dimensions to it, but I am sure that one of them relates to the work of the Spirit in recalling to our minds all the good things that the Father has done for us in Jesus. Maybe the Psalmist knew something of the same power of God within his life:

'Praise the Lord, O my soul,
all my inmost being, praise his holy name.
Praise the Lord, O my soul, and forget not
all his benefits' (Psalm 103.1, 2).

Praise is the platform from which faith operates. It is the antidote to unbelief and ingratitude. The more we take time to let the Holy Spirit have a rummage around our spiritual innards the more we will realise how much we have for which we must praise God. Praise lifts God high within our experience. It puts him in his rightful place and we begin to see everything else in our lives in relation to his greatness. It is the recollection of the mercies of God that prevents us from operating in prayer with a God that is too small (with apologies to J. B. Phillips!). Before we ever get to intercession we need to have our imaginations transposed out of their normal mood into the expectation of spirit that comes from realising afresh all that God has already done.

The Holy Spirit brings to mind those causes for thanksgiving.

Recollection leads to thanksgiving, thanksgiving leads to the exercise of praise. Praise is not only singing. Praise is what leads to singing in the Spirit. It is a liberation of heart into gratitude when we realise and feel all that God has done.

'Praise the Lord, O my soul!'

P. T. Forsyth, in his book *The Soul of Prayer* put the whole thing into perspective:

'Praise and adoration of his work in itself come before even our thanksgiving for blessings to us. At the height of prayer, if not at its beginning, we are preoccupied with the great and glorious thing God has done for us for his own holy name – we are blind for the time to ourselves – we cover our faces – and cry, 'Holy, holy, holy, is the Lord God of hosts' ... Our hearts glorify, we magnify his name, his perfections take precedence of our occasions.'

The Spirit does not leave it there! He begins to light up the whole of our life so that we see everything we are and have in the light of God's goodness. Even things that we have taken for granted, or previously imagined that we earned by ourselves, we discover come from the good hand of God.

We begin to realise with James that,

'Every good and perfect gift is from above, coming down from the Father of the heavenly lights, who does not change like shifting shadows' (James 1.17).

This second movement of divine initiative in our praying lifts us away from ourselves to our Heavenly Father, who has put all this at the heart of our experience. When we have been taken this way and our hearts have been filled with thankfulness, we are ready to bring our requests before God. As Paul puts it:

67

'Do not be anxious about anything, but in everything, by prayer and petition, with thanksgiving, present your requests to God' (Philippians 4.6).

(c) *Motivation*

This is where the truth expressed in Romans 8.26 begins to find its full outworking, for if we don't really know how to pray, it is equally true to say that we often don't know what to pray.

A great lesson to be learned about prayer is that it is about making one's heart and mind available to God for his use.

There are deep things that in this life we will never understand about this aspect of prayer, but those who know from their own experience just what God can do with a heart that is open to him witness to the power of the Spirit on this level of prayer. They know that it is good to come with our known requests before God. It is a good habit to have a prayer list and to know in advance those things that we have to pray about, but, when the Holy Spirit begins to motivate us in the area of intercession, he takes us away beyond all our previous preparations. There is a mystery about this because often those Christians who are used in this way never get to know the whole story of why or how it was that God used them. It is enough to know that he did, that in his grace he used their prayers to fulfil his purpose here on earth.

Andrew Murray, in his book, *The Ministry of Intercession*, attributes high value to this kind of praying. In fact, he says that one of the chief things God is looking for on earth is 'intercessors', men and women who will open their lives before him so that he can impart into them the longings of his own heart. It is the failure of God's people to open themselves out to his Spirit in this way that is the cause of such a lack of spiritual power in the world.

'He has taken them up into partnership with Himself; he has honoured them, and bound himself, by making their prayers one of the standard measures of the working of his power. Lack of intercession is one of the chief causes of lack of blessing.'

A clear example of this occurred some time ago within our own family. My wife, Hilda, got up one morning and felt very strongly that she should spend time in prayer of intercession for a young girl whose story she had heard in the television news. The girl's name was Annabel Schild and she had been kidnapped by bandits in Sardinia. The whole family had been abducted and then the father had been released to raise the ransom for the release of his wife and child. After a while his wife was set free but the bandits held on to the child. Hilda rose with the strong impression that she was to spend time praying for that young girl. She had no idea how to pray and asked God to guide her as to what she should pray for. The date of February 3rd kept coming to her mind and she felt that what she had to do was to read her devotional reading book, *The Daily Light*, for that date. When she did she discovered that it was full of promises of God's protection. It said that God was light and in him was no darkness at all. As Hilda read these verses she realised that although the little girl was perhaps at that moment sitting in a very dark cave with no light, God was there and he was surrounding her with his divine protection.

Hilda then began to praise God that he had Annabel in his protection and to pray against any evil designs the bandits might be plotting against her. Right throughout that day she continued in prayer for the girl until near the end of the day when she met a very dear Christian friend. This friend announced to Hilda that a strange thing had happened that morning. She too had felt constrained by God to spend the day in prayer for Annabel Schild. They then saw clearly that God had probably laid the plight of this girl on the hearts of many Christians and this was the way by which he was going to help her. They agreed to carry on praying, but now for her release from her imprisonment.

For the next two days they pored over the papers and listened for news of the family but there was not a mention of the Schild family on any news media. The temptation was to give up and imagine that they had been fooled by their feelings.

Suddenly on the Saturday morning, three days after they had felt constrained to pray, news broke that Annabel had been found safe and well. Before she left Sardinia for England, Annabel was interviewed by Anna Ford of ITV. One of the last questions she was asked was whether she had prayed during her captivity. Her reply was very interesting. A few days before her release she had prayed because she had heard that people prayed in that kind of situation.

More than one book could be written to illustrate this principle that God uses the hearts and minds of intercessors to fulfil his purpose. It is not something that can be explained at the rational level, but it is something that is experienced at the level of faith.

To realise that the living God is calling us into partnership with him in what he is doing all over the world is surely something that lifts our ideas of prayer out of the dull and ordinary into the realm of life and faith!

Motivation leads to intercession and intercession leads to understanding – the understanding of faith *that sees that God is at work* and that he has chosen to work through the channel of hearts and minds that are open to the promptings of his Holy Spirit.

(d) *Communication*

The real dynamism of prayer can be felt when we understand that it is a two-way exercise. We feel astonished when we realise that God has actually said something to us!

At the end of Romans 11 Paul asks the question in an echo of Isaiah 40:

'Who has known the mind of the Lord?
Or who has been his counsellor?' (Romans 11.34).

The answer comes through another part of his writings, 1 Corinthians 2:6-16. Only through the activity of God by his Spirit within our spirits can we share in the mind of God:

'For who among men knows the thoughts of a man except the man's spirit within him? In the same way no one knows the thoughts of God except the Spirit of God. We have not received the spirit of the world but the Spirit who is from God that we may understand what God has freely given us' (1 Corinthians 2.11–12).

Many times, as we minister to people, we need to rely on what God says directly to them. Many times it takes that kind of word from God to undo the harm that has been done or the fear that has been spread by the Devil. It is only when God breaks through with his directive word that faith is created, and failure or fear reversed.

Not long ago we were ministering to a couple. The husband had a debilitating illness that they were sure would eventually lead to his death. They lived under the shadow of that fact and many other fears had developed in their lives as a result. We felt that the only thing that would bring freedom would be a direct word from God. They were surrounded by the good advice of many friends and counsellors but often that advice was conflicting and the result was spiritual confusion and despair. They felt guilty and no longer knew how to prepare or for what to prepare themselves. For two days we waited before God for that word. In a time of prayer and fasting Hilda felt that one word was impressing itself on her mind and that word was 'life'.

At the end of a meeting, a day or so later, I was asked to pray with this couple without any idea of what Hilda was feeling or what she had said. As I stood to pray with them I heard very clearly within my mind some words of Jesus which come from the story of the raising of Lazarus:

'This sickness will not end in death'
(John 11.4).

I have rarely felt words so vividly and the strength of them almost rocked me back on my feet. At that time I was not expecting such a clear word from God but the results of it were immediate! I had to withdraw for a moment to consult with Hilda and was amazed when she told me of the word she had received from God. Both words together confirmed what God was saying.

When God communicates his word in this way it puts us in a much more profound position of responsibility than if we had never received a direct word from him. In a later chapter I have spelt out the implications of this.

When God communicates his word to us it leads to assurance within our hearts. Assurance of the word of God leads us to the knowledge of what is the right course of action to take. It is the fulfillment of the word that is given through Isaiah:

'As soon as he hears, he will answer you. . . . Whether

you turn to the right or to the left, your ears will hear a voice behind you, saying "This is the way; walk in it"' (Isaiah 30.19, 21).

3. The purpose of prayer

If we were to say any one thing about prayer, we would say that prayer is the means by which God has chosen to release the power of heaven on earth. Through prayer the Holy Spirit makes real to us all that God is, all the power that he has at his disposal and all the blessings he wants to give us in our lives.

As we pray the Spirit works in us in a number of different ways. He brings:

(a) *Refreshment to our spirits*

We often come to prayer with a tired spirit or bearing concerns upon our hearts that cause us to feel heavy or out of sorts. Prayer puts everything into God's perspective; it helps us to see things from his point of view. Often in our waiting before the Lord it is not the problem that changes but our attitude towards it. In the words of Isaiah 40.31:

'Those who hope in the Lord will renew their strength.
They will soar on wings like eagles;
they will run and not grow weary,
they will walk and not be faint.'

God is in the business of restoring our souls. As we wait in his presence we discover within the deep reaches of our beings that inner peace and assurance that comes from knowing who is in control. Paul emphasises the same fact when he urges us to bring all our requests to God with thanksgiving:

'And the peace of God, which transcends all
understanding, will guard your hearts and your minds
in Christ Jesus' (Philippians 4.7).

(b) *Direction to our lives*

It is significant that two of the most crucial words of direction in the early Church came through the experience of waiting on God in prayer. Peter had gone alone to pray when the Lord intervened directly by means of a vision. Through that vision and the word that it communicated, Peter's whole attitude towards non-Jews within the Church was completely changed and the Gospel was opened up to the Gentile world. Many of us today are the beneficiaries of Peter's obedience to that word of direction from heaven.

The other occasion was when Paul was praying and received a vision from God of a man from Macedonia. That vision, and the direction it brought, altered the whole course of Paul's missionary journey and turned him from the east towards the west. Again, that was an act of obedience to the voice of God that was to have far-reaching repercussions in the experience of the Christian Church from that day until now.

God wants to give direction into our lives and he can do that when we take time to wait before him to hear his voice apart from the many other voices that claim our attention.

(c) *Provision for our needs*

Repeatedly in Scripture, believers are assured of the fact that God knows what they need in order to fulfil his will and that he will provide it. I don't believe for a moment that this truth permits the belief that Christians will always have everything they want or, indeed, that they should always expect the best of everything. To go through life carrying the sort of baggage that encourages possessiveness, the sort that we can't bear to leave behind, surely militates against the call to be a pilgrim.

No, what our Father promises is that he will meet every need that will enable us to fulfil the purpose of his kingdom!

'Seek first his kingdom and his righteousness, and all these things will be given to you as well' (Matthew 6.33).

The tremendous fact is that God does not deal with us according to the measure of our need but according to the measure of his wealth. We have behind us all the security of the inexhaustible supply of God!

'My God will meet all your needs according to his glorious riches in Christ Jesus' (Philippians 4.19).

(d) *Victory in spiritual warfare*

The fact is that as Christians we live in a battle-zone! Our whole life is one of engagement with the enemy. We need to recognise this fact of life for, if we fail to live in the light of it, the Devil will be able to overwhelm us. This is where prayer is so important! Of all the weapons God has made available to us within the arena of spiritual warfare, prayer is the most effective.

Two aspects of prayer are important:

The importance of praise

Paul Billheimer in his book *Destined for the Throne* puts it like this:

> 'Satan is allergic to praise, so where there is massive, triumphant praise, Satan is paralysed, bound and banished.'

Sometimes we think there are special tricks in prayer with which to deal with Satan. This leads to a sort of spiritual magic. The fact is that every Christian believer has at his disposal the power of the kingdom of God. Praise is the key to success against the Devil.

The power of intercession

Through intercession God baulks the designs of the enemy. In Ephesians chapter 6, after listing the various parts of the Christian armour, Paul exhorts the readers:

> 'Pray in the Spirit on all occasions with all kinds of prayers and requests' (Ephesians 6.18).

Prayer releases the power of God into a situation. Paul underlines the effectiveness of this weapon of warfare when he says:

> 'We do not wage war as the world does. The weapons we fight with are not the weapons of the world. On the contrary, they have divine power to demolish strongholds' (2 Corinthians 10.3, 4).

(e) *Fellowship in faith*

In that same chapter in Ephesians, chapter 6, Paul speaks about taking up the shield of faith. That is a very vivid picture if we understand what he meant by it.

When the Roman infantry went against a walled city to take it, they did not go as individual soldiers. They used large shields that stood the height of a man. These protected them against the arrows and fiery missiles that were launched against them from the ramparts of the city.

When they approached to attack they marched together in companies. The men on the left put up their shields on the left of the company; those on the right put their shields along their right sides; those in front put their shields along the front. So the sides and front were protected. The men in the middle linked their shields above their heads and covered the whole group. Like a great tortoise they marched forward against the enemy. As long as they kept their shields up together they were safe. That exercise provided cover for other troops to raise their own means of attack against the city walls.

It is like that in the fellowship of prayer. Strength in faith comes when we link together the shields of faith and we discover the strength of being bound together in prayer.

'I tell you that if two of you on earth agree about anything you ask for, it will be done for you by my Father in heaven. For where two or three come together in my name, there am I with them' (Matthew 18. 19, 20).

Before moving on to the next chapter, pause for a moment. Use what you have just read as a check-list for your own ideas on prayer.

Ask yourself at least these three questions:

1. How important do I reckon prayer is to every other area of my life and work as a Christian?

2. What do I expect the Holy Spirit to do within me when I take time to pray?

3. What am I expecting to happen in my life as a result of prayer?

5: Practice makes ... prayer!

*'Have faith in God ... whatever you ask for in prayer,
believe that you have received it, and it will be yours'
(Mark: 11.22, 24).*

I never did like algebra! That was simply because I never
understood it. I never took the time to get to grips with the
principles and so the further I went the more confused I
became. It's like that with prayer. We often don't progress in
prayer because we never take time to think of the principles
that stand at the heart of it. That's what we were exploring in
the last chapter. When we know how God works and what we
can expect, it releases us into new areas of faith.

This chapter is about what we do when we pray. It explores
a few of the principles of prayer in action to enable us to move
forward in our daily relationship with God.

1. The fellowship of prayer

We were driving home one night from a university mission
meeting. It had been a hard meeting and we all felt drained in
spirit. There were about seven of us in the minibus and the
further we drove towards home the deeper was the feeling of
depression inside the bus. We had the feeling that we were the
only Christians on the face of the earth and that the whole
burden of the kingdom had fallen on our shoulders!

We decided to pray. Suddenly as we prayed a great thought
struck us. Someone in the team read the words from Hebrews
chapter 12:

'You have come to Mount Zion, to the heavenly

Jerusalem, the city of the living God. You have come to thousands upon thousands of angels in joyful assembly, to the church of the first-born, whose names are written in heaven' (Hebrews 12.22, 23).

The chapter goes on in a magnificent way but it was those words that did it! Our spirits rose as we realised what they were saying. The Holy Spirit used them to counteract the feeling of despondency and loneliness in the work of God. We had come to realise within our experience a fundamental principle of prayer:

(a) *When you pray you are expressing the fellowship of all believers*

It was a tremendous experience to feel within our hearts that what we were involved in as we came before the throne of grace was something that was the common heritage of believing men and women and angels, not only in that moment of time, but right down through all the centuries of faith. As we prayed we were being joined in faith by all those who had gone before.

This awareness of the reality of the communion of the saints is something that we have lost to a large degree in much modern Christian living. Because we are in a society that lives for the present, we often forget the truth of eternal life as it is found in the communion of the saints. In that moment, in that minibus, we felt as though we were being joined by all the great men of power in prayer and that our words were being echoed in the heart of the great apostolic evangelist, Paul himself.

This is a truth we need to learn, because even in the privacy of our own private praying we are not alone. Jesus said:

'When you pray, go into your room, close the door and pray to your Father who is unseen. Then your Father, who sees what is done in secret, will reward you' (Matthew 6.6).

He did not mean that we would be alone in our praying. He himself promised to be with us always, and always to give us the help of the advocate, the Holy Spirit. Jesus said this to

77

counteract the exercises that were being passed off as prayer but were really only vain shows of the Pharisees' egotism.

It is amazing who you meet behind your closed doors in prayer! You become aware of the presence of the Father through the Holy Spirit. You become aware that you are part of a great army whom God has prepared to enter into the spiritual warfare of prayer in a way that the world would probably regard as foolish and naive. Be encouraged when you pray, for what you are doing is expressing the fellowship of believers, making real in your own experience the communion of all the saints in heaven and earth.

It is in the place of prayer that you will find yourself having fellowship with believers with whom such fellowship might otherwise be totally impossible here on earth. If, like myself, you have travelled, say, behind the Iron Curtain, and met with believers who are not free to come and join with you at home, then you will know the joy of being aware that you all meet before the same throne of grace in the power of prayer.

(b) *When you pray you are expressing the truth of the priesthood of all believers*

When God created the world he made man to be in communion with him. His design was that there should be a never-ending circle of communication between heaven and earth, God with man and man with God. It was that circle that was broken by the disobedience of Adam and Eve in the garden. Ever since, the circle has risen no higher than man's own estimate of himself. Instead of worshipping God, man worshipped himself and created things. He,

'exchanged the glory of the immortal God for images made to look like mortal man and birds and animals and reptiles' (Romans 1.23).

It is a common view amongst those who study comparative religion that man's search for God has always been on the up and up. It is held that in the early days of man's life on earth he was an animist and polytheist who worshipped the phenomena of nature and a great number of personal tribal deities. Under this view the great religions of the world are the end of this search – refined, sophisticated versions of the primitive religions.

The Bible, on the other hand, teaches that in the beginning man was able to communicate directly with God, that he needed neither priest nor altar, and that his life was marked by a close fellowship with his creator. All this changed when man was deluded into thinking that he was as important as God himself and so began to worship things other than his creator. Now and again that first state of affairs is recovered in the lives of great men of God. Abraham is an outstanding example. He had direct fellowship with God and was called away from the worship of idols.

In Jesus, God's ideal in creation has been recovered for all who live by faith in him. When we come before God in prayer we are able to come to him directly with every other intermediary out of the way. The exciting thing to remember when you pray in the name of Jesus is that this brings you directly into the presence of the living God himself! This is because:

> 'there is one God and one mediator between God and man, the man Christ Jesus, who gave himself as a ransom for all men' (1 Timothy 2.5, 6).

Here is an even more exciting thought! Because our relationship with God has been restored, we are now able to act in prayer on behalf of the whole world and people in it. God has made us a kingdom of priests:

> 'To him who loves us and has freed us from our sins by his blood, and has made us to be a kingdom and priests to serve his God and Father' (Revelation 1.5, 6).

It is through our prayers that the circle between heaven and earth is being restored!

(c) *When you pray you are expressing the reality of sonship through the Holy Spirit*

Paul speaks of the work of the Holy Spirit in this respect in Romans chapter 8:

'By him we cry, "Abba, father". The Spirit himself testifies with our spirit that we are God's children' (Romans 8.15, 16).

That is a tremendous thought. When we take time to wait before God, he speaks that truth into our hearts. That is why one of the results of prayer is a new assurance in our hearts of the love of God and of his power, because there we are in touch with our Father.

Paul goes on to spell out the implications of that for our lives:

'Now if we are children, then we are heirs – heirs of God and co-heirs with Christ' (Romans 8.17).

It means that as we come in prayer we are not expecting our prayers to be answered according to the measure of our resources or efforts but according to the riches of the Father because he has made us his children and heirs. All our prayers are brought to the immensity of his resources of power and grace. One of my favourite texts in the New Testament is that simple couplet that Paul uses in 1 Corinthians 3.21, 23:

'All things are yours ... and you are of Christ, and Christ is of God.'

What a supply line!

If we realise just what is involved when we start to pray, that it is much more than just something that we, by ourselves, are involved in, then our whole approach and attitude will be different when we come before God.

2. The pre-requisites of prayer

Effectiveness in prayer is more likely when we get to grips with some of the fundamental facts about the exercise of prayer. We often identify prayer with saying words and, of course, you can't pray without using words, whether they are words in your native tongue or words given to you in a special prayer language by the Holy Spirit. It is during prayer that the gift of tongues comes alive for many Christians. That is particularly so when it is difficult to know just how to pray or what to pray for. Sometimes we need to make ourselves available to God to such a degree that he can pray through us by the Holy Spirit.

There is a great mystery about this. All I can say is that God has chosen to make prayer the means by which he releases his power here on earth. There are times, I believe, when he wants to do a particular work that goes beyond our capacity either to understand or achieve.

Praying is more than using words. There are certain important things to learn as we come to pray:

(a) *It is an attitude of our whole life*

Paul tells us to 'pray continually' (1 Thessalonians 5.17). I am sure that he did not mean that we were to walk about praying out loud. That might be counter-productive in some circumstances! I am sure that he was speaking rather about an attitude of life. The believer is on twenty-four hour call for God! His spirit is always open to the nudging of the Holy Spirit and the lines are always open between himself and God. This means that at any time throughout a day God can stimulate his spirit in intercession. As the experiences of life and the world pass through our lives each day so they become the content of our praying.

P. T. Forsyth put the same thought well when he said:

'Pray without a break between your prayer and your life. Pray so that there is real continuity between your prayer and your whole actual life.'

This is not an excuse to stop taking times alone in the quiet with God. Rather it is the means by which the quiet times will be filled with significant content. To the person for whom prayer is the attitude of a whole life there will never be the lack of something to pray about in the quiet before God!

(b) *It is a necessary part of our discipleship*

It follows that prayer is of the utmost importance both to God our Father and to the world in which we live.

As far as the old prophet Samuel was concerned, failure to come before God in prayer on behalf of others was nothing short of sin.

81

'As for me, far be it from me that I should sin against the Lord by failing to pray for you' (1 Samuel 12.23).

We will feel the real value of our praying when we understand its importance to God and for men. Leonard Ravenhill underlines this when he says in strong words:

'We may call prayerlessness neglect or lack of spiritual appetite, or loss of vision. But that which matters is what God calls it. God calls it sin. Prayerlessness is disobedience, for God's command is that men ought always to pray and not to faint. To be prayerless is to fail God, for he says, "Ask of me."'

(c) *It is an exercise that will cost us something*

Romans 8, the very part of Scripture that speaks of our inheritance in Christ Jesus, reminds us, too, of its corollary within our lives:

'We are ... heirs of God and co-heirs with Christ, *if indeed we share in his sufferings in order that we may also share in his glory*' (Romans 8.17).

What is happening when we pray is that we are making our hearts available to God so that he might lay on us all the burdens of other people. To live in the power of the Spirit is to be taken away beyond ourselves into the needs of other people. Often it seems necessary for us to wrestle with God before blessing can be released.

In a dramatic encounter with God, Jacob discovered this fact. For ever after he bore in his body the mark of this encounter. He wrestled with God right through the night until the dawn, so that he was sure that he would not go away from God's presence without knowing God's blessing.

'When the man saw that he could not overpower him, he touched the socket of Jacob's hip so that his hip was wrenched as he wrestled with the man. Then the man said, "Let me go for it is daybreak." But Jacob replied, "I will not let you go unless you bless me"' (Genesis 32.25,26).

It is often a very painful thing to bear the burdens and needs of other people on our hearts before God. The Devil wants you to feel overwhelmed by a sense of hopelessness and inadequacy, but the intensity of that struggle needs to be measured against the greatness of the power of God and his promises to you.

(d) *It often calls for perseverance*

It is in the very chapter of Luke's Gospel in which we read of the invitation of the Father, 'Ask and it will be given to you', that we also read of the need for perseverance in our praying. There Jesus tells the story of the friend who arrives at midnight to ask for bread. It is only his persistence that causes the man to get up out of bed and meet his request (see Luke 11:5–8). It is in the context of this kind of asking that Jesus issues his invitation to ask so that it may be given. Thus, this is the kind of asking he wants to teach his disciples about.

It is difficult to say why God wants us to be in this position. There is no doubt that it has more to do with us than with him. Often it is our attitude to the problem that needs to be changed, and as we go on praying, we find that our approach to the subject alters in all kinds of subtle ways. Often it is our sense of timing that needs re-adjustment. What we thought was of the utmost priority is seen in the light of God's timing to be less urgent. Sometimes, I think, it takes time to show us the exact measure of the problem involved. We start praying at one level but as we persist we are shown in our spirit that there is much more to the question than we had first thought. One thing is clear, God wants us to persevere so that he can release what he wills into our lives.

Some words of John Wesley, that sound quaint to our ears nowadays, make the same point:

'Storm the throne of grace and persevere therein, and mercy will come down.'

(e) *It is an exercise that depends on faith*

Time and again Jesus made that point. Faith, living trust in the power of God, is what turns prayer from being a meaningless exercise into the secret of divine power:

'Have faith in God .... Whatever you ask for in prayer, believe that you have received it, and it will be yours' (Mark 11.22,24).

Prayer is not faith in faith. It is faith in God and there is every reason for the believer to put his trust in God. After all, God has planted within his experience and at the centre of human history the greatest encouragement to faith the world has ever known. God has not left us to sit and work up faith! Faith feeds on Jesus. Faith looks at what God has accomplished in Jesus. Faith sees the sheer magnificence of what God has done and realises that everything else fades into insignificance beside this:

'He who did not spare his own Son, but gave him up for us all – how will he not also, along with him, graciously give us all things?' (Romans 8.32).

3. The demands of prayer

'When you pray, go into your room, close the door and pray to your Father, who is unseen. Then your Father, who sees what is done in secret, will reward you' (Matthew 6.6).

The approach of Jesus was devastatingly simple! Nevertheless, Jesus shows that if we are to discover the effectiveness of prayer we must pay a cost. This is a cost that many of us are unwilling to pay, for Jesus spelled out the heart of prayer in terms of a relationship between a Father and his son. A relationship demands time – time spent in listening and talking. So we need to:

(a) *Take time with God*

The words of Psalm 46.10 are very relevant here:

'Be still and know that I am God.'

It is when we take time to be apart with God that our spirits can be tuned in to what he is saying. Then our many other interests take second place and there is a chance for him to become central in our lives.

In the early days, taking this time with God proves to be a very difficult discipline, but, as we discover the value of doing it, what at first was hard will become something which we cannot live without.

The first effect of waiting in the presence of God will be felt in the deep areas of our own spirit:

'Those who hope in the Lord will renew their strength. They will soar on wings like eagles; they will run and not grow weary, they will walk and not faint' (Isaiah 40.31).

There are three main reasons why stillness in God's presence is important.

(i) *It removes distractions:* our modern lifestyle brings a lot of hassle into our hearts. Even when we are quiet on the outside the rush still goes on within. It takes time to feel the peace and calming influence of God's stillness. We need to let the Holy Spirit minister to our own spirits something of the peace of God.

(ii) *It provides opportunity for meditation:* the best thing to do is to start with a simple prayer asking God to make his presence real to you. Then use some verses of scripture or some simple spiritual help like *The Daily Light* or one of the more modern equivalents. The important thing about this is that whatever you use it must be the word of Scripture that your mind is being focussed on and not somebody else's discussion about Scripture. What you are doing is allowing the Holy Spirit to work in your spirit and letting the word of God have its effect in your mind.

It is no good just trying to empty your mind and be quiet. As soon as you vacate it of one set of ideas, another will be standing by to rush in and take the place of the first. The mind needs to be filled with something of God and focussed on his thoughts.

(iii) *It allows inspiration of our spirits by the Holy Spirit:* prayer is not just about what we want to say to God. Central to

85

prayer is what he wants to say to us. Often the first way he speaks is through Scripture. The Holy Spirit will take the words of the verses you have read and through them will begin to reveal thoughts about God to you.

So take time to wait. Find the time of day that suits your schedule. Some of us protest that we can never find any time, what with the family and the demands of a busy modern life. That usually means that we haven't looked too closely at our priorities or at those odd moments we tend to let flit away between the more important occasions of the day. Half an hour is what is needed in the first instance so that there is time for concentration to develop and preparation to take place.

(b) *Be definite in prayer*

Jesus' words are unequivocal:

'Whatever you ask for in prayer, believe that you have received it, and it will be yours' (Mark 11.24).

Half the problem about unanswered prayer is that we quite often don't know what the question was. Faith is taking God at his word! Throughout the New Testament we are encouraged to ask God directly for our needs.

'You do not have, because you do not ask God. When you ask, you do not receive, because you ask with wrong motives' (James 4.2, 3).

Two instructions are laid down for us in Scripture with regard to asking in prayer:

(i) *Be simple*

'When you pray, do not keep on babbling like pagans, for they think they will be heard because of their many words' (Matthew 6.7).

Some people find it all too easy to surround their requests with so many words and so much pious jargon that the simplicity of our requests becomes hidden. This is one of the

86

things that prevents some Christians from sharing their prayers with others. They are afraid that they will appear silly and naive in front of some of their fellow Christians who have a facility with words.

Speaking in straightforward language to God helps us to develop a feeling of contact and intimacy with our Father in heaven.

(ii) *Be specific:* Paul puts it clearly when he says:

'Do not be anxious about anything, but in everything, by prayer and petition, with thanksgiving, present your requests to God' (Philippians 4.6).

God wants to hear what we are asking. When we pray in vague and general terms we cannot know where to look for the answer. So many liturgical prayers in church services are meaningless to the hearers because the words are not specific. To pray for 'all missionaries' and 'all those who are sick' may seem on the surface a very commendable thing to do, but it fails to make the point for most people. I believe that non-Christians would be much more impressed if they heard the Church committing itself to specific requests. Our faith becomes more personal as we speak about personal and particular things in our prayers. Of course, that calls for more faith because there is always the risk, from the human angle, that what we are praying for won't come about, at least as we would like it to.

When we ask God for something in prayer, we are putting faith into action. God knows what we need before we ask. This is what Jesus taught his disciples according to Matthew 6.8:

'Your Father knows what you need before you ask him.'

Why ask then? We do it because our asking is a demonstration of our trust in him. We ask as children who trust their Father. Never to ask is never to trust.

Make a list of the things you ask God for so that you will remember what you have asked and when you asked. That is important for the next step.

(c) *Expect God to answer*

The answer to our prayers will come in a great variety of ways. The answer may come in a way that is quite different from anything that we expected, but if we pray believing, God will answer! It is important to look for answers.

The Devil manages to discourage us, sometimes, when it seems impossible that our prayer will be answered or the answer is very slow in arriving.

Nowhere is the sense of miracle more real than in the area of answered prayer. For myself, it is because the issues involved are so down to earth. They involve real people and actual circumstances, and when you see these things being affected before your eyes it creates a sense of wonder and amazement at what God can do!

Some time ago we were leading a mission and on the first night the local minister introduced a young woman to my wife. This woman was suffering from severe anorexia nervosa and her marriage was on the rocks. Only the previous night she had taken an overdose of drugs. Hilda tried to speak to her, but the girl seemed impervious to help and advice. Hilda went home feeling completely deflated, as though she had failed totally. She wanted to pray for the girl and her husband but had no idea where to start. As she prayed in tongues the Lord challenged Hilda about how much she could believe for this girl. Hilda agreed in her heart that she could muster enough faith to believe for a smile on the girl's face.

The next night the girl turned up at the mission meeting and she smiled! That encouraged Hilda to look for something more in faith. She decided to pray that against all the odds the girl's husband would come to one of the meetings. The next night the husband turned up at the meeting with his wife! His response was cool, but it was enough to encourage Hilda to go on to the next step of faith and pray for an opportunity to speak directly to them. Much later, after the meeting had ended, Hilda went through to the coffee lounge to discover the pair there and she was able to speak with them.

That encouraged another faith-step and she prayed that God would really be allowed into their lives. It was not until the very last day of the mission, the day Hilda was due to return home, that the girl came up to her and opened up in a totally new way. She admitted God had been speaking to both her and her husband throughout the week. Later that day they opened their lives completely to God and found a new beginning together in the power of the Holy Spirit.

Such experiences teach us that God will start where we are. If we are honest with him, he will take our faith and build on it. As we see him answer one request, so our faith increases and we learn to trust him for more and more.

(d) *Share faith with others*

'How good and pleasant it is when brothers
live together in unity!
It is like the precious oil poured on the head,
running down on the beard,
running down on Aaron's beard,
down upon the collar of his robes.
It is as if the dew of Hermon
were falling on Mount Zion,
for there the Lord bestows his blessing,
even life for evermore' (Psalm 133).

The two vivid and lovely metaphors of Psalm 133 remind us of the value of meeting together to pray and to worship God. The oil with which the priest was anointed was an offering of a sweet smell to God. The dew of Hermon was the source of refreshment on the ground for man. There is a tremendous benefit to be gained when Christians join with other Christians in the practice of their prayer.

(i) *Encouragement:* the writer of the Hebrews exhorted his hearers to the same end:

'Let us not give up meeting together, as some are in the habit of doing, but let us encourage one another – and all the more as you see the Day approaching' (Hebrews 10.25).

It is a helpful thing for your own development in prayer if you can meet together with someone else who will build up your faith. Sometimes we give up praying simply because of the pressure of being alone. Our faith wavers and before we know where we are it has disappeared. When the faith of one person is under attack then the fellowship of others can be a great source of strength and encouragement.

If your circumstances make it impossible for you to meet with another Christian, then a valuable alternative in building your faith is to read some of the biographies of the great men and women of prayer: people like E. M. Bounds, Andrew Murray, Hudson Taylor, Leonard Ravenhill, John Hyde, Campbell Morgan, George Mueller, Charles Finney, John Wesley and William Wilberforce, to name but a few.

To share faith and the results of faith with other Christians is one of the greatest faith-building exercises you can indulge in.

(ii) *Agreement:* Jesus spoke time and again of fellowship in prayer. He saw the united prayer of two or three believers as having great power in the service of his kingdom.

'Again, I tell you that if two of you on earth agree about anything you ask for, it will be done for you by my Father in heaven. For where two or three come together in my name, there am I with them' (Matthew 18.19, 20).

To know that others are standing in faith with you in a particular situation brings strength and a sense of commitment into your own praying. It is easier to keep your own appointment of faith with God if you have entered into a covenant with someone else to do that. This is where the telephone can be such a helpful tool in the battle of faith, particularly amongst housewives who are perhaps unable to travel to meet each other because of home commitments. A word on the phone can be the means of raising prayer very quickly in an urgent situation.

(iii) *Enrichment:* when he speaks about spiritual gifts, Paul underlines the benefit we bring to each other when gifts are exercised within the Christian fellowship:

'Now to each one the manifestation of the Spirit is given for the common good' (1 Corinthians 12.7).

Often direction or encouragement can be brought to a

group of Christians in prayer through the exercise of particular gifts of the Holy Spirit. Our understanding of how to pray or what to pray for is often enhanced by the exercise of the spiritual gift of knowledge or prophecy. The mutual exercise of spiritual gifts educates the prayer of faith, and is one of the most helpful aspects of sharing together in prayer.

(iv) *Engagement:* nowhere is sharing in faith more important than in the realm of spiritual warfare. It is here undoubtedly that strength is gained from joining together in prayer. It is where he speaks of spiritual warfare in Ephesians chapter 6 that Paul is careful to bring his injunction:

'Pray in the Spirit on all occasions with all kinds of prayers and requests' (Ephesians 6.18).

Nowhere are we more exposed to the attacks of Satan than here. Yet this is the heart of prayer. It is the battle zone where the kingdom of light and the kingdom of darkness confront each other.

(v) *Discernment:* John counsels us to test every spirit to see whether it is from God or not (1 John 4.1). So many things happen within the realm of our mind and imagination that it is always necessary to pass our thoughts through the sieve of the Holy Spirit's testing. One important way that this happens is within the fellowship of other Christians. It is important to expose those thoughts and impressions that we think are of God to the scrutiny of other Christians who can look and listen objectively and put them to the test.

There is nothing to be afraid of in doing this for if what we have heard in our time of waiting is really of God it will be confirmed and strengthened rather than threatened.

(e) *Develop a capacity for prayer*

Prayer is about growth. The more time we take to pray, the more capable we will become. Grow in prayer:

– *by overcoming moods.* Don't go on feelings! There will be days when prayer seems far from you. Keep on praying and you will find that God's power in your prayer is not affected by how you feel. P. T. Forsyth puts it succinctly when he says:

'Do not say, "I cannot pray, I am not in the Spirit."
Pray till you are in the Spirit.... If you are averse to
prayer, pray the more.'

– *by extending vocabulary.* I don't mean that we need to
learn more words. We need to develop confidence before God
so that we can tell him exactly what is on our mind. Our
prayer language takes time to develop and we need to relax in
spirit as the Holy Spirit leads us into the language of
intercession through the use of tongues.

– *by increasing faith.* I have already shown how God takes
us step by step in the building up of faith. It might be helpful
to start with a prayer list so that we can be definite in our
praying. However, the Spirit will lead us off the end of our list
into further areas of his concern. As we observed in the last
chapter, the motivation of our intercession is one of the main
tasks of the Spirit within us.

– *by developing ministry.* Prayer, in its widest sense, is the
calling of every Christian. But special ministries of prayer are
also given to individuals. It may be a ministry of intercession,
or of healing, or a burden of prayer for some other special
calling. As we go on developing in our prayer life it becomes
clear to ourselves and others just what this may be.

– *by trusting judgments.* The more we pray, the more we
come to recognise how God works in us. Whereas at the
beginning we may be very hesitant, and rightly so, to put too
much weight on our responses and the judgments we make in
the light of them, the more we mature, the more we are able to
trust ourselves in these areas. This is a hallmark of maturity in
prayer. With increased ability to express our prayers and faith
to believe them, there comes the gift of discernment which
enables us to respond correctly to inner impulses and
impressions.

If you want to put this into practice, here is a simple
prescription to follow:

1. *Find time for God*

Choose a time in the day that suits your life. You will need
half an hour or so to begin with. Personally, I feel the principle
of tithing is important here. We recognise generally that when
we tithe we give ten per cent to God. But not just *any* ten per

cent. The principle of the firstfruits demands that it be the *first* ten per cent! There is good reason for this. If the first ten per cent is given to the Lord it will greatly affect how I use the other ninety per cent. So it is with prayer. If the first thing I do in my day is to spend time with the Lord, then everything else in the day will be affected by that fact.

This tithe of time makes room for God in all my time!

2. *Stimulate your mind with Scripture*

Start by reading a passage of Scripture and meditating on it. Alternatively, use a set prayer or a hymn that is based on Scripture.

3. *Pray aloud*

If you say your prayers out loud it will:

(a) concentrate your attention and save your thoughts from wandering all over the place.

(b) develop confidence in the sound of your own voice. It is sometimes fear of our own voice that prevents us sharing in prayer with other Christians.

4. *Make a list*

Note the things or people you want to pray for and look for answers to your prayers. Also, make a note of those items that were brought to you by the Holy Spirit *during* your prayer time.

5. *Keep on praying*

Don't be put off just because you don't feel like it. Make time at least once every day and keep the appointment with God.

6. *Trust God*

' "Test me in this," says the Lord Almighty, "and see if I will not throw open the floodgates of heaven and pour out so much blessing that you will not have room enough for it" ' (Malachi 3.10).

7. *Find someone with whom to share your prayer*

Even if it is not possible to meet together regularly, build a faith-line between yourself and at least one other Christian.

6: Seeing the invisible

' "The days are coming," declares the Sovereign Lord, "when I will send a famine through the land – not a famine of food, or a thirst for water, but a famine of hearing the words of the Lord" ' (Amos 8.11).

We were in a prayer meeting in Wimbledon. Hilda and I had never been there before and most of the people were complete strangers to us. We were there because we were staying overnight in the home in which the meeting was being held. We had come to London from Durham because we had become aware that God was moving us on to a new sphere of work. We needed direction and help and had come to London to meet with some leading figures in certain parts of the Church. For all our talking, the two days had been frustrating and fairly pointless. So we went back to Wimbledon.

The prayer meeting continued with praise and intercession. Suddenly, towards the end, a woman at the other side of the room began to speak. She was describing a picture she had been given in her mind. The picture was in two parts. In the first she was standing on the terrace of a large country house looking out over finely laid gardens. Everything was neat and tidy and according to plan. The scene led her gaze out to the end of the garden where she could see a copse of trees in which stood a building. When she looked more closely, she discovered to her chagrin that the building was not real. It was a folly built only for decoration. The second picture was just as vivid. This time she was in the middle of a thick wood. She was in a clearing but there was no obvious way through the wood in any direction. The strange thing, however, was that sunlight was beaming through from above into the clearing and she had a fantastic feeling of warmth and security. She felt the picture had some particular significance to someone in the meeting.

You could have bowled us over. I had never before experienced God speaking in such a direct and personal way. That vision went right through us and we have dwelt on it time and again because that is precisely what God was saying and that is precisely what he has done. He was telling us that our way forward was not within the normal channels of planning and security, that we had not to look in the obvious places for direction and help. We had to trust his love and although the way seemed difficult and impossible at times, we were to stand in the light of his presence.

That experience opened up a whole new dimension for me. Up until that time I firmly believed that God could speak, but I was never quite clear how, beyond reading verses in the Bible, I would be able to perceive what he was saying. Now I believe that God speaks in the present tense. I have also came to see that, if we are to hear him clearly, then certain things must be true within our experience. One of the great problems we face today is that there are many people who believe that God speaks, and are open to that, but who to a great extent ignore the preconditions that enable them to hear him much more clearly and without the risk of being led astray by other voices.

How, then, are we to hear the voice of God? How does God impart that faith-vision into our lives that will direct us into his will? I believe that there are certain important factors to be taken into consideration:

1. The Revelation of his Word

'Faith comes from hearing the message and the message is heard through the word of Christ' (Romans 10.17).

One of the sad features of many contemporary 'renewal' meetings is the absence of the word of God – and by that I mean the Bible! Frequently I find myself wanting to speak from the Scriptures with a group of people only to discover that a great number don't carry a copy of the Scriptures with them.

The two things for which Jesus lambasted the Sadducees of his own day were just this: 'You do not know the Scriptures nor the power of God' (Mark 12.24). There is a direct link between the two. It is through the medium of Scripture that we understand the nature of God. It is through the medium of Scripture that we perceive God at work. It is here that we can live with him for here he lives with us. Through the Scripture we can see his operation in the lives of many different sorts of people. We can see his purpose being unfolded. Through the Scripture we can begin to understand the creative power of the word of God. The more we live in the Scripture the more aware we become that we are handling something that is beyond mere history or theology. It is a living, creative, powerful force that breathes life and creates judgment. Ignorance of the Scriptures can, in the end, only mean ignorance of God, because it is here that he has chosen to reveal himself in a way that is far more particular and extensive than anywhere else.

We can learn of God elsewhere, for example, through the beauty of creation, but that is like learning about an artist through his work without ever actually meeting the artist. We will come to know something of his skill and his technique and his signature, but of the depths of his own being and the reaches of his personality we will remain in the dark. What we need to do is meet the artist, talk with him, listen to him, share in the burdens of his heart. God has made that possible for us through the Scripture. *It is nothing short of a revelation of himself.*

Now if we want to be able to hear God's voice, we need to start here.

There are two major reasons why this is so:

(a) *God knows that we need direction*

The Devil's interest is to divert us from God's will for our lives. The way to resist that is to live under submission to the word of God and so have our lives built on a true foundation. He makes the Scripture live so that we will hear it with a new authority and want to live in the light of it.

(b) *He does it to teach us a principle*

He brings his word alive in our hearts to teach us that this is where life is. When we became Christians it was not the eloquence of the preacher or the singing or laying on of hands that brought new life, it was the creative word of God. Then after we have become Christians, faith continues to live within our hearts by the continued application of the word of God. When God speaks something always happens.

The trouble with most of us is that we impose ourselves upon the Bible. We come to our reading of it with our presuppositions and ideas, and usually with the tools of the trade already in our hand. We come with our Scripture notes or commentaries, ready to dig another chunk of gold for our latest sermon or a verse 'to do us good'.

What we need to do is let the Bible come to us, let it impose itself on us. When we open ourselves to the word of God in a submissive way things can happen within our minds and spirits of which we were up till then unaware. It will have its effect. It will touch the deep parts of our spirits and flow through our minds and bring challenges and controls within our lives in a way that no other approach can. Most of us only ever 'Bible-study'. What God wants us to do is to wait *before* the word and let it have its effect on our hearts.

The power of the Scripture operates in a number of different ways within our experience:

(i) *Infiltration* – we need to learn the art of meditating before the Scriptures, of taking a translation that we are happy with, that we can get to grips with, and of letting the word settle into our hearts and minds and seep into the deeper parts of our personality.

> 'Blessed is the man who does not walk in the counsel of the wicked.... But his delight is in the law of the Lord, and on his law he meditates day and night. He is like a tree planted by streams of water, which yields its fruit in season and whose leaf does not wither. Whatever he does prospers' (Psalm 1.1-3).

Start by taking one part of Scripture, for example, one of the shorter psalms.

Sit quietly. Before you start to read say a short prayer. Ask God to release his word into your spirit. It is not a matter of looking for a verse to do you good, or even of finding an outline for your next sermon. What you are doing is waiting before the scripture. Through it God is working in your inner heart so that in a later moment you will find that the power of the word will come to your mind and affect your thinking and your actions.

'As the rain and the snow come down from heaven and do not return to it without watering the earth and making it bud and flourish, so that it yields seed for the sower and bread for the eater, so is my word that goes out from my mouth: It will not return to me empty, but will accomplish what I desire and achieve the purpose for which I sent it' (Isaiah 55.10-11).

The most important thing we need to discover about the Bible is that it is a living creative force which can work with great effect in the deep reaches of our lives and experience.

(ii) *Education* – through our exposure to the Scriptures we are made aware of the workings of God.

'All scripture is God-breathed and is useful for teaching, rebuking, correcting and training in righteousness, so that the man of God may be thoroughly equipped for every good work' (2 Timothy 3.16, 17).

It seems to me that a great part of our present difficulty in perceiving the voice of God lies in this area. There has been a general ignorance of Scripture which has led to an even greater ignorance of the ways of God. Scripture does not just throw ideas about God at us in a vacuum but interprets them within the context of real-life experiences. We can see God at work within human life. We can understand what he requires of men and how he deals with them. We can see how he speaks and understand the inflections of his voice. If our hearts and minds have been trained through the medium of Scripture it is much more likely that we will be at home with his voice when he chooses to speak through other means such as faith-picture or prophetic word.

(iii) *Illumination* – the greatest thing of all is when we hear the word of God through Scripture.

'Open my eyes, that I may see wonderful things in your law. I am a stranger on earth; do not hide your commandments from me' (Psalm 119.18, 19).

It is no accident that for many people the first thing that changes when they are renewed in the power of the Holy Spirit is their awareness of the Bible. Before it had been dead for them. Now it lives with new power. What previously had been largely a source of information, now becomes the vehicle of the living and directive word of God.

There should be no surprise about that, since it is the same Spirit who inspired the word in the first instance who now brings inspiration in to our hearts to make it live again and again for us.

2. The sanctifying of our minds

'Do not conform any longer to the pattern of this world, but be transformed by the renewing of your mind. Then you will be able to test and approve what God's will is – his good, pleasing and perfect will' (Romans 12.2).

The Devil knows the importance of our minds. In Christian circles we speak a lot about heart and spirit, but what goes on in our minds is of vital significance. Capture a man's mind and you affect his actions and his whole life. Marcus Aurelius, the Roman philosopher, put it succinctly: 'A man is dyed the colour of his thoughts'. That's the principle the ad-men work on. If a seed can be planted at mind level then it will affect our actions when we next think of buying something.

Minds are dangerous places:

(a) *Fearing our minds*

There are, of course, parts of our minds of which most of us are afraid. Those are the deep areas where imagination rules and in which the secret movements of our being take place. Many Christians are afraid of the realm of imagination, and for good reason.

Yet it is in the realm of imagination that God wants to work. He wants to revitalise our imagination and use it for his purpose, not only so that we may think good thoughts about creation, art and culture, but because he wants to communicate with us within the realm of our imagination. He wants to use our minds, which he has created, as receptors for his word.

When Paul speaks about the renewal of the mind I don't think he means just the intelligence, the cognitive part of my mind, but all that is involved in mind, including the deep reaches of the subconscious. Everything that is my mind needs to be renewed by God, not only so that I can use my mind as I reach out towards him, but so that God can use my mind in the movement from him to me.

As I have said, however, there are deep reasons why many of us, as Christians, fear our minds.

(i) *They are the realm of the sinful.* For many of us the real spiritual battle takes place not in the realm of the actual, but in the realm of the imagined. The Devil has a field day there. It is there that lust rules supreme. It is there that guilt breeds. It is there that we do battle with the raw and basic elements of our nature and fear looms large. So imagination has to be overcome. The sad fact is that in attempting to control it we often negate it and so live our lives at the very pedantic level of the literal and legalistic.

(ii) *They are the realm of the impossible.* There we dream up our impossible fantasies. The Devil creates castles in the air which have no chance of becoming real. Faith is replaced by pipe dreams which bring depression and frustration in their wake. We have a proper caution about letting our minds run away with us, but the result is often negative. Maybe that's why so few of us are at ease with the arts. How our appreciation of beauty has become stultified under the impact of a repressed imagination!

And yet it is just here that the Holy Spirit wants to deal with us. To have 'our minds renewed' means something much more dynamic than thinking good thoughts about God. Surely it speaks of the recovery, through the redemptive power of Jesus, of a part of our being that has become negated under the impress of so much legalistic and dull religion. God means us to function at the level of imagination!

In fact, it is one of his power-houses within our spiritual experience, if only we could release it for his use.

Oswald Chambers spoke of the same need when he said:

'The test of spiritual concentration is bringing the imagination into captivity ... one of the reasons of stultification in prayer is that there is no imagination, no power of putting ourselves deliberately before God ... Imagination is the power God gives a saint to posit himself out of himself into relationships he never was in.'

Because we recognise our fears, however, many of us try to stifle the imagination. We attempt to stay out of that part of our inner house. We try to tame our imaginations instead of finding victory within them. We could live in a large place within our minds. We may live in very restricted conditions in the outside world but our minds need not be small. However, because we have stifled our imaginations, our world has shrunk, our personalities have been diminished and our religion has been damped down until it has become scribal and pedantic.

It is here that what I have said about Scripture is very important. Scripture disciplines our minds and fills them with the right things. It is no good just sitting down and trying to clear the mind of all the things that are in it. We need to take time to be still, to allow the Holy Spirit to bring us into focus with God. One of the best ways to do that to begin with, is to take a Bible verse or a short passage of Scripture and use it to focus the mind on. Or we can take a Scripture-song which brings us into God's presence. The Scripture or the song need to be of the sort that speak about God. They make us aware of him and of what he does. Then we will find that other thoughts are moved to the side and our minds are centred on that one thing. That practice alone is vital. As we practise taking time to think with God we gradually gain the ability to stop at any time in the middle of a hectic life and train our minds on God. That 'God-focus' is essential if we are to experience the renewal of the mind.

(b) *Filling our minds*

The other thing we need to be careful about is what we fill our minds with. One of the things the Holy Spirit wants to do in our lives is develop in us a gift of discernment.

There are many wholesome, creative features about God's world which are to our benefit, which we can enjoy, and which will enlarge our appreciation of life. By the same token there are many things presenting themselves to us today that are unworthy of their name of art, culture, or education. It is little wonder that we have difficulty in the realm of the imagination when we are willing to let it be permeated with so much rubbish.

I had an interesting experience not so long ago. Two people came to speak to me. They were very uptight and both had a problem with inner freedom. I discovered that they both had the same hobby: they had a passionate interest in Nazi war crimes. All their spare time was spent reading of the atrocities that had taken place under the Nazi regime during the Second World War. Their imagination had been fired and captivated by the obscenities that filled this literature. I had to tell them to go home and burn the lot. Until that happened and until their minds were cleared of the debris that such reading left behind, there was no way in which the Holy Spirit could have control of their imagination.

Paul put it clearly when he said:

'Set your minds on things above, not on earthly things' (Colossians 3.2).

A mind filled with such rubbish cannot be under the discipline of Jesus because there are other things commandeering it. The world is full of two things – *good* and *bad*. If you want to be on the side of God you need to learn to choose the good. Ask the Holy Spirit to develop in you the gift of discernment that is his barometer of righteousness.

I recall one time not long after we had experienced that new touch of God's power. We switched on the television to watch a favourite comedy programme. It had only been on a few minutes when both Hilda and I realised that it was no longer to our taste. It is not that there is anything intrinsically wrong with television, it was just that this particular programme seemed to be more full of cheap smut than we had remembered!

Sometimes when I am away from home with members of the team we look around the shops of the town where we are. Somebody might see an article and suggest that I buy it for Hilda. In a second or two I can say whether or not she would like the article. Why is this? It is because I know her very well. I have lived in her life for twenty years and she in mine. We know each other's likes and dislikes intimately. If I take something home for her it is most surprising if she does not like it.

Suppose Jesus lived in us to that extent. Is it not logical to think that we would be able to tell what he would like or dislike?

When we set our minds on things above it means we identify by the Spirit of Jesus those things that find their source in him. It means we concentrate on what comes from him, what reflects his glory, and what would be pleasing to him. Many of those things won't in themselves be religious things but they will bear his stamp of creative goodness.

> 'Every good and perfect gift is from above, coming
> down from the Father of the heavenly lights, who
> does not change like shifting shadows' (James 1.17).

The devil wants us to ignore our minds or, at least, to use them in a limited way. He is not too concerned if all we are doing is filling our minds with information, even religious information. Much modern education runs at that level. Even theological education today tends to ignore the deeper reaches of mind. It stuffs us full of facts but fails to teach us how to make our minds available to God.

Yet God does not want us to use our minds simply at the level of logic, and the analysis of information, important though that is. We need to make them available at every level so that he can communicate through them to us. He wants to release our imaginations into his service.

It is in the realm of faith-vision and direction that God can most creatively use our imaginations. He can direct our thoughts and plant into our minds his thoughts and purposes. Through the channel of our imaginations God can communicate his ideas to us. As we wait prepared before him he can use our imagination as his print-out terminal. The Old Testament is full of instances in which God did precisely that. This is not a by-passing of the mind, or the subjugating of personality. It is the outcome of co-operation between a mind that has been willingly sanctified before God and the mind of God himself.

Neither does it rob us of responsibility. Rather, it places us in a position of even greater responsibility, for when the word of God is heard and received, it calls for obedience at a deeper level.

We don't need to be afraid of what God will tell us in our minds. The idea of faith-pictures or direct revelation scares some people. There is good reason for that, because Satan is the master-counterfeiter and he can just as easily plant ideas if we are not careful to prepare ourselves in the right way. When God speaks, however, he never uses only one witness. The faith-picture of which I spoke at the beginning of this chapter has become foundational for all our life and ministry only because it was part of a whole range of witness. When God speaks through such faith-pictures, he will verify them by other means, perhaps by Scripture, or the witness of other Christians, but it will certainly not stand on its own.

3. The fellowship of believers

The communication of the word of God is a gift to the body of Christ. That has been the safeguard of the Church since the beginning. 'No man is an island,' said John Donne, and nowhere is that more true than in the realm of the Spirit. We are born of the Spirit into the fellowship of the people of God.

The communicative gifts of the Spirit – wisdom, knowledge, discernment, prophecy, tongues, interpretation, teaching, and so on – are given to the Body. They operate through individuals but for the good of the whole Body. That is what Paul says in 1 Corinthians 12.7. The Good News Version catches the idea well:

'The Spirit's presence is shown in some way in each person for the good of all.'

The word is heard, tested, and obeyed within the context of the body of Christ. Even a word of particular direction for an individual needs to find that echo of witness and consent amongst the members of the Body.

I recall hearing an illustration years ago about guidance. It was taken from the experience of the crews of motor torpedo boats in the English Channel during the Second World War. They patrolled the English coast watching for prowlers and carrying out rescue missions. The inshore waters were laid with mines and it was a precarious business finding the way back to home port. The plan was quite simple, though. On the shore were posted three telegraph poles. The captain aligned these poles with the help of his binoculars so that only one was visible to him. Then he headed his boat for the shore in the knowledge that he was following the swept channel that was clear of mines. Those three telegraph poles, kept in line, saved him from fouling one of the dangerous sea mines that had been laid to prevent the enemy from landing.

So it is with listening to God. There are signposts within the fellowship of believers. Three important spiritual safeguards are given to us within the context of the body of Christ. Perhaps these are areas where the Church has most to learn about encouraging openness and mutual care between the members of the local fellowship.

(a) *Submission*

For some this is a dangerous term to use. It carries for them overtones of heavy authoritarianism and the denial of personal liberty. It should not be so. We should not allow the abuse of a good spiritual principle to divert us from the fact that we all, as Christians, need the covering of fellow believers in our daily lives. Every Christian needs to be in a place of listening with other Christians. This threatens some of us. What it means is mutual submission within which we can listen together and test our own perceptions of what is being heard. In that way we can discover the richness of fellowship and save ourselves from the dangers that go along with strong-headed individualism.

(b) *Sharing in faith*

Jesus said:

'If two of you on earth agree about anything you ask for, it will be done for you by my Father in heaven' (Matthew 18.19).

The idea of agreeing in faith is powerful. It is also a protection against the hurried-ness of spirit that the Devil wants to breed within our lives. Often we want to rush ahead and ignore the advice and fellowship of other believers. There is nothing to fear if what we are testing is really a word from God. His word endures for ever and faith grows from faith.

It is within the context of sharing faith that the Holy Spirit is free to operate through the complementary gifts which he distributes in the lives of Christians. Quite often, having heard God speak to us in one particular way, we will meet with other Christians only to find that God has spoken the same word through the fellowship in quite different ways.

Some time ago we were quite sure that God was telling us to move from the situation we were then in and set up the right kind of base for the team ministry in which we are involved. We heard that chiefly through an inner conviction of spirit and the testimony of the Scriptures. Not long after we were taking part in a conference at The Hayes Conference Centre in Swanwick, and we shared part of this conviction. To our amazement and joy God put a picture of the house into the mind of a fellow United Reformed Church minister who was at the conference. A year later, when we moved into that house, we were able to see how God had printed into the mind of that brother a faith-picture of the very house that we eventually purchased! The more amazing thing is that, at the time the picture was given, we had not even the remotest idea of what part of the country we would eventually settle in, let alone what house we would buy. Today we live in that house!

(c) *Strength in fellowship*

When Paul speaks in Ephesians 6 about the operation of faith it is within the context of the body of Christ:

'Take up the shield of faith, with which you can extinguish all the flaming arrows of the evil one' (Ephesians 6.16).

With the word of God often there comes doubt. That may seem a contradiction in terms but it is the Devil's intention to rob us of the word. His interest in life is to strip the word of its power. He does that by sowing discouragement and doubt in our minds. He throws a question-mark against the word of faith. Just as he did at the beginning, so again he addresses the question to us: 'Did God *really* say . . . ?' (Genesis 3.1)

The thing that saves us when we are under that kind of attack is the fellowship that comes from sharing faith with other Christians. Paul exhorts us to make that our aim in our life with one another:

'Therefore encourage one another and build each other up' (1 Thessalonians 5.11).

This is why we have moved within the Bethany Fellowship. We have discovered that to be effective in the work that God has given us, we need to minister from within a context and atmosphere of faith. To one degree or another that is true for every Christian. Loneliness is the greatest threat to our spiritual welfare.

4. Hearing the word

There are three first steps that we can take to help us hear the word of God more clearly:

(a) *Take a look at Scripture*

Take a selected passage.

Sit quietly and ask God to make the Scripture live within your mind and life.

Read the passage in a relaxed way so that you can grasp what it is saying.

Read it through a number of times prayerfully, letting your mind rest on those parts which the Holy Spirit highlights as you go through.

Let your mind focus on the thoughts that God brings through the Scripture to you.

Learn to go on from there with praise for the word, opening

your mind to be stimulated by the Holy Spirit in praise and prayer.

Ask God to release in your own spirit the gifts of his Holy Spirit that will help you to hear and understand his word.

(b) *Take a look at the main interests of your life*

Carry out a review of what you are feeding into your mind:

What kind of books do you read?

What kind of conversations do you indulge in?

What sort of television programmes do you watch?

What kind of leisure pursuits do you indulge in?

Will all these enrich you personally and direct your thinking towards good? Or are they the kind of things that will encourage your imagination away from goodness and God?

(c) *Take a look at your friends and fellowship*

Do you have friends who encourage faith?

Is there anyone with whom you pray regularly?

Are you able to share with other Christians your hopes and difficulties in your Christian life?

Who would you turn to for spiritual direction?

The answer to all these questions is important for it will determine, in the end, whether we are able to receive God's word within our lives.

7: Living in the vision

'The secret things belong to the Lord our God, but the things revealed belong to us and to our children for ever' (Deuteronomy 25.29).

I was lying face down on the sitting room floor. The previous few months had been marked by regular attacks of asthma that had sapped my physical energy and had caused spiritual exhaustion.

A few weeks earlier a Christian brother had been introduced to me and, amongst other things, he was a gifted physiotherapist. His gift became the means of a great deal of relief and healing. On this particular night he was giving me the treatment and finding parts of my anatomy that I never knew existed. It was fairly painful! In the middle of all this he stopped and announced suddenly that he had received a word from the Lord for me. He told me that he believed that the Lord had given me a vision for the future of my ministry and went on to say that what I was to do was to take this vision to the throne of grace.

At the time it seemed a very strange word, but a few weeks later I found out exactly what it meant. What this friend did not know at the time was that I was living with a new sense of direction in my heart for the whole future of the work and ministry. At that time we were looking for the right house in which to base the team and to provide the kind of accommodation for the various team members.

Four weeks later we found the very house we needed. The only trouble was that it cost eighty thousand pounds and we didn't have a penny. We met together to fast and pray and to let the vision be tested in fellowship with each other. It was then that the word came back to me about taking the vision before the throne of grace. Suddenly it made sense! My whole inclination was to get out and about and try to do something about raising the cash. Surely there were avenues we could explore and steps we could take to secure some mortgage cover? Still the word came back that we were to take it to the throne of grace.

We discovered through experience that there are a number of different levels at which God begins to fulfil the word that he gives into our lives.

1. It is fulfilled before the throne of grace

From a rational point of view it seems almost naive to suggest that we should do nothing but pray. Yet that is exactly right. There are a number of important reasons why this is so:

(a) *God's word is conceived in his own heart*

The principle of Deuteronomy 29.29 comes alive within our experience when we trust God. If God has a word for us, however it may be imparted, one thing is sure, *it is his word before it is ours!*

What the devil wants us to do is to treat it as though the word were ours and as though we had, therefore, to fulfil it in our own strength. Christians receive many words from God but never wait before God with them. The result is confusion and hassle as people try to bring God's word to pass within their lives in their own strength.

(b) *God's word is confirmed by waiting in his presence*

Over the weeks of waiting with the vision of the house that we believed God was providing an exciting thing happened. The more we brought the vision before the throne of grace, the more we were confirmed in that vision. Time and again we heard the word of divine approval about the project of faith.

One of the things we need to develop in the practice of our faith is a theology of failure. What happens if what we think we have heard doesn't happen? It is so easy to live in fear at this level and to dread the possibility of embarrassment in front of other people. That is why we should not be hasty to make claims on behalf of God before we have heard the divine 'Yes' of approval. The fact of the matter is that if what we are hearing is not the will of God it will not come to pass unless, by some spiritual jiggery-pokery, we manipulate things and bring something to birth in the name of faith that does not belong to God.

What we need to do is live with the vision. Through prayer and fasting and fellowship we need to bring the vision continually before the throne of grace. If we have a 'Yes-word' from God it will grow in strength and conviction and there will be increasing confirmation of the rightness of the course of action.

(c) *God's word is accomplished first in heaven*

The Scriptures witness time and again to the power of God to fulfil his will and to hear our requests.

'If we know that he hears us whatever we ask – we know that we have what we asked of him' (1 John 5.15).

'If two of you on earth agree about anything you ask for, it will be done for you by my Father in heaven' (Matthew 18.19).

We need our faith-vision fulfilled in God's presence before anywhere else. Once God has confirmed it and has released the supply, no power on earth can touch it.

Perhaps we were pushed to the point of leaving our house entirely with God, because the project was far too big for us to achieve at any human level, but with God all things are possible! There is no threat in taking a vision to the throne of grace because there it can only be refined and grow.

'Though it linger, wait for it; for it will certainly come and will not delay' (Habakkuk 2.3).

The spiritual value of waiting with the vision before the presence of God cannot be counted too highly. Oswald Chambers makes the same point when he says:

'We always have the vision before a thing is made real.

111

When we realise that although the vision is real, it is not real in us, then is the time that Satan comes in with his temptations, and we are apt to go down. Instead of the vision becoming real, there has come the valley of humiliation.

'God gives us the vision, then he takes us down to the valley to batter us into the shape of the vision. And it is in the valley that so many of us faint and give way.'

This is where the exercise of prayer and fasting and thanksgiving is so important. We need to polish the vision up. We need to have to have it made real again to our hearts. We need to allow the Holy Spirit to bring faith to birth in our hearts so that we can withstand the negativism of the Evil One.

2. It is realised in the progress of events

The Scipture is full of promise:

'My God will meet all your needs according to his glorious riches in Christ Jesus' (Philippians 4.19).

Recently we have had some building work completed in the house. I learned a lot about planning regulations through that experience. Before you can start, all the plans are inspected and then authorisation slips are issued. The work proceeds at the speed of the authorisation. When one stage is completed it is inspected and then work can proceed to the next stage. So it goes stage by stage until one day you stand in the completed whole.

It's a bit like that with faith. When God moves you, he moves according to the release of his will. Alongside the confirmation of God's word in your heart will come some evidence of progress at the level of supply. The first thing that happened with us was a cheque for ten thousand pounds. It was a few weeks before any other material sign was given but that was the first stage release that God used to support the confirmation in our hearts. This trust and waiting on God allows our faith to grow –

– *it recognises that provision belongs to the Lord.* The reason why faith is so blunted today in many quarters is that

112

we have ceased to trust God absolutely. Many churches today are suffering from the faithless prudence of by-gone generations. The future of the church and church property was seemingly secured by the investment of trust funds so that the whole show could be supported by the interest. The net result has been that second and third generation members have never had to exercise real faith and many places of worship are still kept open with a handful of faithful, but dispirited worshippers, when they should have been closed long ago.

The Devil wants us *active*. He is never happier than when we are involved in frenetic activity and caught up in the hassle of trying to do things in our own strength. Then he can sap our energy and divert our vision. Instead of seeing the possibilities of faith we see the impossibility of the situation.

We need to learn to live in the faith-promises of God, to ask the Spirit to release to us from the Scriptures all the great words of faith. We need to live like Abraham:

'He did not waver through unbelief regarding the
promise of God, but was strengthened in his faith and
gave glory to God, being fully persuaded that God had
power to do what he had promised' (Romans 4.20, 21).

– *it admits the final test of prophecy*. In the book of Deuteronomy we read of two tests which should be applied to all prophecies to discover whether or not they are really the authentic words of God (Deuteronomy 18).

Firstly the prophet had to speak words that were consistent with given revelation. That is always a necessary hallmark of true prophecy. Prophecy never contradicts Scripture and never adds anything to the revelation given in Jesus. It brings the word of God in directive power for now.

Secondly, the prophetic word has to come to pass. There is little point in our making claims to have direction and words from the Lord if there is no prospect of them coming to pass. I remember clearly once being involved in a foolish boyish prank. I was away from home for a prolonged period and at a strange school in a town near the seaside. In an attempt to impress some new schoolfriends I recall spinning a yarn about some rich uncle with a yacht who would be calling to see us in the harbour one day. With great gusto I issued promises by the score of free trips aboard the vessel. It went so far that we actually went one evening to the top of the harbour wall. It was dark and blustery. I remember peering over the estuary with such enthusiasm for the appearance of this make-believe yacht that I almost convinced myself of my own lie. Of course, there was no hope of it coming true and I knew it. To recover face I had to invent yet another falsehood.

I sometimes wonder if our approach to faith isn't a bit like that. Do we deal in pipe dreams or in the realm of God's reality? The men who receive God's word don't live in a world of fantasy but of *faith which comes to pass!*

'Faith is being sure of what we hope for and certain of what we do not see' (Hebrews 11.1).

The reason why faith needs to be tested before God is because ultimately it needs to be tested before men. Far better that we be found lacking in our spiritual perception in the presence of the Father who can redeem all things and give us new direction, than appear fools in the sight of men who will not be slow to dishonour the name of God.

– *it holds us to God's timetable.* I am coming to believe more and more that God has a perfect time for almost everything within our lives. That is not fatalism, it is faith! Fatalism leaves things blindly to a god who is unknown in terms of personal trust and experience. Faith is being open to a Heavenly Father who has a perfect care for our whole life. Faith is life lived in co-operation with its creator.

To believe in, and live in, God's timing is to be in the position of fulfilling his will rather than our own. God's way of holding us to his timetable is very practical. He releases the supply according to the measure of his will. An army on the advance can only move as it establishes lines of supply. When, there's a war, the chuck wagons never go in first; the fighting troops are in there and their supplies come up behind. It's like that with faith.

Not long ago I listened to a programme on the radio about the island of Spitzbergen in the Arctic. One interesting feature was about how the hunters prepare in the light summer days for their forages into the dark Arctic wastes in winter in search of their quarry. During the summer they walk around their hunting area planting supplies of food every few miles. In the winter when they are hunting they know that the supply is out there ahead of them. Faith is not like that. It goes in the assurance that God will provide but in the knowledge of risk because there is nothing up ahead. We can go as far as the present provision takes us and then faith needs to be active for the next step.

We now take it for granted that if something is provided by God in advance it is because the Lord is aware of a need that is about to break on us unawares. Recently we had an experience that underlines this principle.

We were praying that the Lord would provide the eighty thousand pounds needed to purchase our new ministry base. Three days before the moving date, he did just that, but then the phone rang and the voice at the other end said, 'You won't remember me.' I confessed that I did not remember the person concerned, until she reminded me of an incident in which I had met her fleetingly a few months before. 'A funny thing has been happening to me,' she said. 'For two or three weeks now your name will not go our of my mind.' Then she went on to tell me that in the last two or three days the reason for this had become clear to her. She had the strong impression that she had to give a gift towards our work. What she didn't know was that we were moving on the following Tuesday.

I felt that it was not right to speak to this person over the phone about such a subject and so invited her for lunch on Sunday. She came and stayed till about eleven o'clock that night. During the day we spoke about the work and shared fellowship together. On the way out of the door she handed me a cheque for twenty thousand pounds!

I explained that the capital sum for the house had been met in a wonderful way but that God surely had particular plans for her gift. It happened like this:

First, we tithed ten per cent of that twenty thousand, which left eighteen thousand. Then we repaid to the bank seven thousand pounds which I had borrowed on a short term overdraft to meet the hefty stamp duty and other fees in the house purchase, plus the removal expenses and so on. That left eleven thousand. When we arrived at the new house we discovered two things. First, a double garage, for which a previous owner had received planning permission, had not been built. Second, when we looked through a trap door in the ceiling upstairs, we found a whole floor in the roof where they were old rooms and fittings which had not been used for years. It needed refurbishment and a new staircase, but then, instead of a two storey house, we would have a three storey house which would be just what the doctor ordered for the team and offices. When we investigated how much all these things would cost we discovered that the garage and the third floor rooms together came to a total of eleven thousand pounds! We remembered the great promise of Scripture, 'Before they call I will answer' (Isaiah 65. 24). Praise God he is a faithful provider, not only faithful in his provision but faithful to his timetable. We need to open our hearts not only to the fact that his promises are faithful, but to the fact that he is faithful in all his ways.

'Every good and perfect gift is from above, coming down from the Father of the heavenly lights, who does not change like shifting shadows' (James 1.17).

3. It is maintained through the exercise of faith

We need to know that to live a life of faith is to live under the onslaught of Satan. His business is to deny the word of God. The word that God speaks into our experience is the word that creates faith. This kind of faith is not something we have naturally – it is a gift from God. It is the same gift of God that brought us our salvation.

'For it is by grace you have been saved, through faith – and this not from yourselves, it is the gift of God – not by works, so that no one can boast' (Ephesians 2.8).

Everything we receive from God in provision or direction is related to what he has done for us in Jesus. Our faith in God is daily upheld and strengthened as we are reminded time and again by the Holy Spirit of what God has done for us in Jesus. When we live in the good of that, we have less trouble believing God's promises about every other need in our lives.

'He who did not spare his own Son, but gave him up for us all – how will he not also, along with him, graciously give us all things?' (Romans 8.32)

116

There are some simple exercises that we can practice to keep the word of God alive within our experience:

(a) *Recite the mercies of God*

One of the things that keeps our faith alive and encourages us to trust God in every new situation is the remembrance of all that he has done for us in previous situations:

'Praise the Lord, O my soul;
all my inmost being, praise his holy name.
Praise the Lord, O my soul,
and forget not all his benefits' (Psalm 103.1, 2).

The recollection of the goodness of God within our experience is one of the most therapeutic agents of faith. In the history of Israel, the people of God were time and again directed to take practical steps to do this. When the people were led through the Jordan by Joshua they were instructed to take twelve stones from the river bed where the priests' feet had stood on the dry ground and build the stones into a pillar of witness,

'to serve as a sign among you. In the future, when your children ask you, "What do these stones mean?" Tell them that the flow of Jordan was cut off before the ark of the covenant of the Lord' (Joshua 4.6, 7).

Again, when, under Samuel, they had routed the Philistines, the spot was marked by a large stone of witness (Ebenezer means 'stone of help').

'Thus far has the Lord helped us' (1 Samuel 7.12).

So we need to note the occasions of God's goodness to us, those times when we have known for certain that God has helped us. Mark them and remember them and they will be a source of strength in those moments of doubt when faith seems hard. *Faith marks the spot!*

The meaning of the words of the old hymn by Robert Robinson have become lost to us because we don't understand their full significance:

'Here I raise mine Ebenezer;
Hither, by Thy help, I'm come;
And I hope, by Thy good pleasure,
Safely to arrive at home.'

These words are not the expression of a wistful optimism but a recognition of all the mercies of God which form the basis for faith. We need to build the pillars of faith within our own experience so that when the Devil comes with his doubts we can take him on a faith tour. As we re-visit the memorials to God's goodness in our lives we will find that the power of the Devil is diminished within our hearts. If there's one thing Satan can't stand, it's the recollection of faith in the lives of God's people! This is a necessary step of obedience. If we sit in depression, it will grow deeper and deeper. It is essential to see thanksgiving as an exercise of obedience. Thanksgiving builds faith. Praise is the platform on which faith is constructed.

(b) *Live by the principle of faith*

(i) *The normal Christian life.* We need to see that faith is the principle by which we live throughout our life here on earth. Faith breeds faith. It is intrinsic to the nature of faith that it leads to the need to exercise more faith. Once we have taken the first step of trusting God and listening to his word we will discover that we need to go on trusting him and listening time and again for his word. God meets our need, not just to satisfy our longings, but to enable us to go on living by faith in him.

The way to keep faith alive is to live by faith. Each step of faith is a step on the pilgrimage: faith is the footstep of the believer.

Many of the problems with which we struggle would never see the light of day if we realised that there was no other way to live. If we refuse to exercise our trust in God in any circumstance we break the chain of faith; doubt and defeat replace the power of God within our experience.

(ii) *The perspective of faith.* It is easy to identify faith with answered prayer. Yet faith is not really bothered about answers to prayers. Faith gets answered prayer but faith is more concerned about the reality of God within our lives than with any particular answer to prayer. Faith releases us from anxiety over problems or a neurotic obsession with ourselves, because it releases us into God. The result is confidence in prayer so that God can release his provision to us, but faith is more than just praying about things. It is bigger than that. Faith is a gift from God. It is creative in me and makes room for prayer to be answered, but it does not depend on that.

Habakkuk, the Hebrew prophet, saw right to the heart of faith:

'Though the fig tree does not bud
and there are no grapes on the vines,
though the olive crop fails
and the fields produce no food,
though there are no sheep in the pen
and no cattle in the stalls,
yet I will rejoice in the Lord,
I will be joyful in God my Saviour' (Habakkuk 3.17, 18).

(c) Learn the language of faith

The Devil wants to convince us that things don't work in the realm of the Spirit. On the surface he seems to have a good case. Here we are, surrounded by all the advantages of scientific research: our cars, washing machines, digital clocks, home computers and audio-visual units. It seems such an absurd thing to tell someone to sit down, shut their eyes and speak to somebody who may not even be there in the hope that he might be able to do something about the profound problems of our living which not all of these material things put together can solve.

Yet that is what faith is saying.

'We fix our eyes not on what is seen, but on what is unseen. For what is seen is temporary, but what is unseen is eternal' (2 Corinthians 4.18).

What we need to do is learn the language of faith. That was the language Jesus himself used to counteract the claims of Satan. When the Devil tempted him he kept saying to him: 'It is written' (see Luke chapter 4). Jesus knew that Satan did not know what to do with that sort of language. The language of faith counteracts the language of doubt.

When someone does not speak your language, he has very little influence over you. He can rant and rave and make all sorts of threats that would bring fear into the heart of his fellow countrymen, but if you don't speak the same language, then those threats have little power. We need to learn God's language and speak it whenever doubt is around.

The Bible is full of the language of faith.

'Blessed is the man who trusts in the Lord, whose confidence is in him.
He will be like a tree planted by the water that sends out its roots by the stream.
It does not fear when heat comes,
its leaves are always green.
It has no worry in a year of drought and never fails to bear fruit' (Jeremiah 17.7, 8).

The word of God is faith-creative. The words themselves bear life in the power of the Holy Spirit and when they are used as an exercise of faith within our spirits they *become what they say*.

How to hear God's word for you

1. Set aside a day in which you are going to fast and pray. Be clear that this does not mean that you will do no work or have a day off work. This simple exercise is possible even within the context of a busy life.

(a) Drink only water through the day, missing out breakfast, lunch and daytime snacks.

(b) Open the day with a time with God. Use a passage of Scripture, such as a psalm, on which to meditate. Start by praising God with song, then move into asking God to speak through that day.

(c) Set specific times aside at regular periods through the day to be quiet and to pray – every hour or two hours for five or ten minutes.

(d) Use what would have been your time for lunch to spend another longer time of waiting on God in meditation and praise. Write down any Scripture, impression, promise or word of direction that God lays on your mind.

(e) Repeat the exercise throughout the afternoon.

(f) In the evening, before breaking your fast with an evening meal, review what you have heard from God. Make specific notes.

This exercise is best followed through in fellowship with Christians with whom you are close, with your family or with those who are waiting to hear God's direction with a common goal in view.

2. When you receive a word of direction follow the suggestions outlined in this chapter:
– keep bringing it before the throne of grace in prayer and thanksgiving;
– speak out the vision before God. Quite consciously give it back to him;
– expect God to do something about the vision.

3. Continue your exercise of faith.

(a) Recollect the things that God has done and praise him specifically for them.

(b) Build up your faith by looking for the next faith-step you need to take. Don't be afraid to be specific. When you know what you are believing for or what you need to hear, it has the effect of building up your faith.

(c) Learn your faith language. Underline in your Bible the words that specially create faith in your own heart. Use them whenever your faith wavers.

Believe God. He can do it!

8: Battle stations!

'The weapons we fight with are not the weapons of the world. On the contrary, they have divine power to demolish strongholds' (2 Corinthians 10.4).

It was Wednesday and the mission we were leading had been going on for four days. The meetings were proving very difficult and had been marked by a strange feeling of resistance amongst the people. It was almost as though there was a wall between those who were leading and speaking and the congregation.

After the staff meeting on Wednesday morning my wife, Hilda, felt that some time should be spent in the church building praying round the pews and at various points in the building. She was the only person free that afternoon and so she spent about two hours in the church, praying for freedom from whatever was causing the resistance in the minds of those who were coming to the services.

That night things were completely different. It was as though everyone had been set free and we experienced tremendous blessing from God in that meeting. We were in the realm of spiritual warfare!

Some people associate the idea of spiritual warfare with the more unusual reaches of spiritual experience, perhaps witch-craft or demon-possession. There is no doubt that warfare takes place there in a very real way, but we need to be aware that spiritual warfare is the context within which every Christian lives. Many of the events and circumstances which we take for granted and look upon as being in the normal run of things are used by the Devil to divert Christians or to prevent the power from flowing through them.

René Padilla, the South American teacher, puts his finger right on the spot when he says:

'Those who limit the workings of the evil powers to the occult, demon possession and astrology, as well as those who consider the New Testament references to these powers as a sort of mythological shell from which the biblical message must be extracted, reduce the spirit of evil in the world to a merely personal experience. A better alternative is to accept the realism of the biblical description and to understand man's situation in the world in terms of enslavement to a spiritual realm from which he must be liberated' (*The New Face of Evangelicalism*).

The New Testament supports this assessment of the human situation. There is no such thing in the world as a free person. If we choose not to live our lives under the Lordship of Jesus then the fact of the matter is that we will live it under the domination of something or someone else. Paul put it like this:

'As for you, you were dead in your transgressions and sins, in which you used to live when you followed the ways of this world and of the ruler of the kingdom of the air, the spirit who is now at work in those who are disobedient' (Ephesians 2.1, 2).

The tendency within the modern, western Church is to dismiss this sort of description as archaic. It comes out of a pre-scientific world in which all the aberrations of human experience were attributed to one spirit or another. Those of us who were educated according to the tenets of modern liberal theology would all, at one time or another, have subscribed to such an 'enlightened' view of life.

The problem is that once the Holy Spirit has come in power into one's experience an awareness soon develops, not only of the reality of spiritual good, but also of the awesome reality of spiritual evil. The fact of spiritual warfare stands at the heart of every real experience of the Holy Spirit. It is not something only to be associated with the fringes of spiritual experience, but is at the very centre of the Christian life. It stands to reason that if men and women *are* in bondage to the power of spiritual evil then it is going to take something of a struggle to liberate them from it.

1. The reality of spiritual warfare

When Paul speaks about this spiritual warfare he is unequivocal:

> 'Our struggle is not against flesh and blood, but against the rulers, against the authorities, against the powers of this dark world and against the spiritual forces of evil in the heavenly realms' (Ephesians 6.12).

Spiritual warfare takes place at three levels:

(a) *Within ourselves*

The fact of the matter is that every one of us is a walking civil war. A battle continually goes on between two sides of our nature. One side wants to do right, while the other seems to be set in the opposite direction. For every resolution that is made to do good there seems to be a determination never to fulfil it. It is Paul again who highlights the intensity of this warfare when he says:

> 'I do not understand what I do. For what I want to do I do not do, but what I hate I do ... I see another law at work in the members of my body waging war against the law of my mind and making me a prisoner of the law of sin at work within my members' (Romans 7.15, 23).

Paul's graphic description of that inner struggle which he cannot understand echoes the experience of us all. It is a vivid description of the often violent struggle that goes on within the human spirit when Satan tries to dominate and impose his authority through our wrong actions.

(b) *In the world about us*

The whole world is a theatre of war, not only in the political and military sense, but in terms of spiritual warfare. An intense battle is being fought among the nations between the forces of spiritual evil and good. There is no other explanation for the folly of our actions at an international level than that mankind is in the grip of some power of evil that drives him towards his own destruction. John spells out the reality of this in his letter when he says:

'The whole world is under the control of the evil one' (1 John 5.19).

Professor F. F. Bruce comments on that verse:

'In the world which God created man has been made in his Creator's image to represent him to the rest of the created world. But man has abdicated his dominion over the world as God's representative in favour of a dominion which he imagines is autonomous, but which in fact has let in the powers of evil and anarchy.'

The result of man's denial of the authority of God in his life and in the world at large has been that he has come under the authority of another, more sinister power.

(c) *In the heavenly places*

It may not be too difficult for us to recognise the reality of what has just been suggested. Yet there is another more profound level of spiritual conflict of which we may be completely ignorant.

A graphic picture of this conflict is provided in the tenth chapter of the book of Daniel. The meaning is hidden to us to a large degree because that is the nature of the book. The intention, however, is clear. While Daniel was praying there was a battle taking place between the spiritual forces sent by God to help him and those who opposed this help. The messenger reported to Daniel:

'The prince of the Persian kingdom resisted me twenty one days. Then Michael, one of the chief princes, came to help me, because I was detained there with the prince of Persia' (Daniel 10.13).

It is clear that the text does not refer to a literal 'prince of Persia' but rather to some personality of evil who had authority within a particular realm. What is clear is that the passage portrays a confrontation that occurs, not within the sphere of our limited experience, but in the broader reaches of spiritual reality.

To see spiritual warfare in these terms helps us as Christians to understand just how seriously we must take the conflicts of spirit that go on within our own lives. They are part of something that is much wider, a great spiritual struggle that embraces the whole of life, spiritual and physical, and which continues every moment between good and evil. It is not an equal struggle because the final downfall of evil and of Satan has already been forecast in the powerful victory of Jesus in the Resurrection. In that event the prophetic word of Genesis 3.15 is magnificently fulfilled:

'I will put enmity between you and the woman, and between your offspring and hers; he will crush his head, and you will strike his heel'.

Three titles are given in the New Testament to Satan that serve to underline the reality of the three spheres of warfare we have looked at. Firstly, he is described as 'the god of this age' (2 Corinthians 4.4), who by subtle means seeks to subvert the interest of men and women. At root he is the source of those conflicts within our spirits that threaten at times to tear us apart. Secondly, he is described as 'the prince of this world' (John 12.31; 14.30; 16.11) who seeks to assert his authority at a global level. Thirdly, he is described as 'the ruler of the kingdom of the air' (Ephesians 2.2).

Of course the limitations of this authority are clearly drawn. The power of the Devil is greatly attenuated because

'the one who is in you is greater than the one who is in the world' (I John 4.4).

The final outcome of the struggles is not in doubt. This is an important fact to bear in mind when we are engaged in a spiritual struggle. The enemy struggles violently because he knows that his doom is sealed. His evil design is to take as many unsuspecting souls as possible with him to share his fate. Just as we can know today the victory of God through the power of the Holy Spirit in us, so God's power will be demonstrated ultimately for all to see in the power of Jesus:

'The kingdom of the world has become the kingdom of our Lord and of his Christ, and he will reign for ever and ever' (Revelation 11.15).

2. The resources for spiritual warfare

Just as it is important to recognise that every Christian is involved in spiritual warfare, so it is essential to recognise that every believer can be equipped for spiritual warfare. Nothing is more dangerous than the view that the ability to engage in spiritual conflict is the gift of a special group of Christians with special secrets of ministry. Paul's concern in Ephesians chapter 6 is to show just how adequately every Christian can be equipped to meet the onslaught of evil.

'Therefore put on the full armour of God, so that when the day of evil comes, you may be able to stand your ground' (Ephesians 6.18).

These words are so familiar that to many of us they have almost lost their punch. Yet when we examine them again we begin to see just how potent they are for us. Take, for example:

Truth. Paul exhorts his readers to stand firm with the belt of truth buckled around their waists. We have to see what he really means. He is not saying that we will be able to stand in a situation of spiritual warfare just because we believe all the right doctrines. The word 'truth' at this point in the New Testament means much more than a set of propositions. For us, truth has come to mean a set of ideas that are either right or wrong. However, the Greek word for truth, *aletheia*, has a much deeper significance than that. *Aletheia* is the ability to see into the heart of the matter. It is the gift of not taking things at face value. *Aletheia* means that we are not fooled by appearances but are able to discern how things really stand.

This is a very important gift for spiritual warfare. Whether it be within the confines of our personal struggle or in the wider reaches of spiritual conflict, the Devil wants us to take things at face value. Often his victory within our own lives is achieved because he plays on our own estimate of ourselves. We appear to be sinful, broken, weak people. At one level that is certainly true but the Holy Spirit is there to help us to look at ourselves from God's point of view. When he looks at us he does not see the weakness of our humanity but the perfection of Christ. He sees less of what we are and more of what he is making us. That is the secret of victory within our own hearts, that we act on God's estimate of things, rather than on the realism that Satan deals in.

In the wider sweep of life *aletheia* is the Christian's radar set. It helps him to pierce through the fog that Satan creates. It saves him from being fooled and enables him to act with divine insight. The New Testament describes Satan as the father of lies and we need the gift of truth through the Holy Spirit to help us combat Satan's delusions.

Righteousness. Another apt description of the Devil is that he is 'the accuser of our brothers' (Revelation 12.10). Nothing is more destructive within our lives than false accusation. We need to stand in the righteousness that is ours in Christ Jesus:

'Therefore, there is now no condemnation for those who are in Christ Jesus' (Romans 8.1).

To be effective, accusation needs to operate between two poles. It requires the pole of invective in the sender and it needs the pole of guilt in the heart to which it is addressed. If contact can be made between these two, then the accusation wreaks havoc. What breaks contact is the blood of Jesus. If we were left to ourselves there would be a great number of grounds for accusation. We need to experience and stand within the righteousness that God brings to us in the power of the Holy Spirit. When it does not meet with guilt in us, the accusation of the Evil One evaporates into insignificance.

'Who will bring any charge against those whom God has chosen? It is God who justifies. Who is he that condemns?' (Romans 8.33, 34)

Peace. Paul uses a very vivid metaphor to drive his point home. He depicts a Roman soldier fully dressed for war. On his feet are the supple sandals that enable him to travel fast and light on the long route marches of war. For the Christian these are the sandals of the gospel of peace. Today, peace usually means the absence of war, but, for the Christian, peace is something that is used in war! This is because the New Testament idea of peace is drawn from the old Hebrew word *shalom*. This does not mean a cessation of hostilities, so much as wholeness, totality or completeness. When something is whole there is *shalom*. When people are at one with each other there is *shalom*.

The work of Satan is to divide. The task of the believer is to be equipped by the Spirit with 'the readiness that comes from the gospel of peace' (Ephesians 6.15) that is, the readiness to heal the breach, to move in wherever the Devil creates division and disharmony with the healing power of the love of God. Peace, in the biblical sense is not a negative thing but a very powerful force for God in a world of division.

Faith. We have looked in an earlier chapter at the power of faith and how our faith needs to be joined with the faith of others. The image of the shield that is used in Ephesians 6 underlines this.

John stresses the same point in his letter. It is our belief in Jesus' power to overcome the world that is the effective weapon in our battle with evil in the world.

'This is the victory that has overcome the world, even our faith. Who is it that overcomes the world? Only he that believes that Jesus is the Son of God' (1 John 5.4, 5).

Faith is directed to what God has already achieved in Jesus. Faith does not whistle in the dark; it sees clearly the significance of what God has achieved on the Cross. To faith, the Cross is not only a demonstration of the love of God, but it is also an affirmation of the power of God! Faith always interprets Calvary through the words of Jesus:

'The prince of this world now stands condemned' (John 16.11).

For the believer, the Cross is God's ultimate declaration of victory. There the crucial battle of the ages was won, everything else that comes after is a mopping-up operation!

129

Salvation. Another of Paul's writings provides the key for our understanding of this rather strange phrase, 'the helmet of salvation'. In 1 Thessalonians 5.8 Paul expands the idea slightly when he says:

' ... and the hope of salvation as a helmet.'

There is the secret! Hope is the weapon God gives us by the Spirit and with this we can withstand the despair of the Devil. Apart from God there is no hope. Outside Christ we are 'without hope and without God in the world' (Ephesians 2.12). In fact, despair is one of the Devil's commonest tools: he keeps men and women in bondage through hopelessness. There is plenty to feel hopeless about – the inner reality of one's own life, the state of society at large, the precarious state of the world situation. Nothing saps the energy quite like despair, but the believer hopes in Christ and that is his strength. Paul puts it like this:

'We do not lose heart. Though outwardly we are wasting away, yet inwardly we are being renewed day by day ... We fix our eyes not on what is seen but on what is unseen. For what is seen is temporary but what is unseen is eternal' (2 Corinthians 4.16, 18).

It is a special work of the Holy Spirit to make the hope of God real within our hearts. It is not something that is gained from watching *News At Ten*. If we go on the evidence of things as they appear to be, then we will not be filled with hope. God needs to enable us to see things from his point of view:

'May the God of hope fill you with all joy and peace as you trust in him, so that you may overflow with hope by the power of the Holy Spirit' (Romans 15.13).

The word of God. The word of God is described as 'the sword of the Spirit'. That was certainly the case in the experience of Jesus. In the throes of spiritual warfare immediately after his baptism Jesus used the word of God with devastating effectiveness. On each occasion that the Devil confronted him, he parried by drawing attention to what God had to say about the matter: 'It is written' (Luke 4.4, 8, 12).

The Devil had no answer against that. We need to learn for ourselves just how allergic Satan is to the word of God. It was here that he won his first victory over man, when Adam and Eve forgot what God had said and listened instead to the Devil.

The general neglect of the Bible throughout the Church today has not only led to vast ignorance of the things of God, but to an incapacity in the area of spiritual warfare. All our arguments about how and why the Bible is inspired must not distract us from the fact that when it is let loose within life it works with dynamic power. We need to argue less and live in it more. The Scripture claims that power for itself:

'The word of God is living and active. Sharper than any double-edged sword, it penetrates even to dividing soul and spirit, joints and marrow; it judges the thoughts and attitudes of the heart' (Hebrews 4.12).

This verse probably applies to more than the word of God through Scripture. It also means that direct word that can be given by other means, for example, through a word of prophecy. Yet the principle holds good, for if God's word is not effective in Scripture it is effective nowhere else.

Prayer. Prayer is not here listed as part of the armour of the Christian, but it it surely the most important factor in this whole scene of spiritual warfare. Prayer is the means by which all the other parts of the armour are applied. In warfare, prayer is the Christian's direct communication with Headquarters!

There are some important points to bear in mind when you pray in warfare:

(a) *It is faith not eloquence that wins God's battles*

Satan wants us to be too aware of the apparent weakness of our prayers. He tries to convince us that nothing can be effected with such feeble words. Don't believe him!

God's ways have always seemed foolish to the onlooker. Right through Scripture the witness is that God achieves his purposes by means which look ridiculous at first glance.

Consider the incident with Gideon in Judges 6 and 7. Three hundred men were set against a multitude and then only with empty jars, lighted torches and a few trumpets!

Think of the occasion when David faced a vastly superior Philistine army. No wonder he didn't disclose his plan of action to his fellow generals, for David was more interested in what was happening in the copse of balsam trees than in what was taking place within the ranks of the enemy. God had assured him of victory, but the way he achieved it seemed to fly in the face of every known tactic of military warfare.

'As soon as you hear the sound of marching in the tops of the balsam trees, move quickly, because that will mean the Lord has gone out in front of you to strike the Philistine army' (2 Samuel 5.24).

Or think of the time when God saved the city of Samaria through the ministry of Elisha the prophet. When Elisha disclosed the fact that God would deliver the city of Samaria by the next morning in his own power, even the allied generals were sceptical. On that occasion God used the wind blowing through the gullies of the surrounding hills to scare the wits out of the Syrians. They became convinced that the noise meant that the Egyptians were coming to help the city and so they high-tailed it out of there as quickly as they could. It was left to four lepers to discover the truth of what God had done.

Just as in Old Testament times God's power was not limited by restricted military resources, so today it is not limited by restricted vocabulary. Only lack of faith limits God.

(b) *Prayer engages us in the purposes of heaven*

The Devil wants us to be overcome by the sheer size of the problem.

A friend of mine had a remarkable experience which illustrates how, through prayer, we are engaged in the purposes of God. One day she met a friend and shared with her how over the past days she had felt a tremendous burden for children in need. She was conscious that the world is full of deprived children and the area where she lives has its full quota.

The friend with whom she was speaking told her that she too had developed a real burden on her heart for the very same thing. One afternoon as she was resting after lunch she received a vision from God. The vision was of an angel coming down and plucking from her mouth the words of her prayer for all these children. He took her prayer, which to her seemed so ineffectual, and deposited it in the bank of heaven.

Such a story seems almost naive. And yet it is the experience of many people of prayer that God does use their prayers in that kind of way. E. M. Bounds once described prayer as 'the capital stock of heaven'. It is as though our prayer becomes a divine research of strength on which the Father draws at times of intense spiritual conflict.

(c) *Prayer releases in us the power of praise*

In his book, *Destined For The Throne*, Paul Billheimer emphasises the power of praise within spiritual warfare:

> 'Satan is allergic to praise. So where there is massive, triumphant praise, Satan is paralysed, bound and banished.'

We read in 2 Chronicles 20 of how Jehoshophat, king of Judah, was taught the power of praise in warfare. He was instructed not to send the fighting troops into battle first but instead to send the choir! The power of the praise of the Levites sent the enemy into such complete confusion that the men of Judah did not even have to lift a sword! Maybe if we understood in our churches what power praise had within spiritual warfare, there would be fewer willing volunteers for any vacant places in the choir!

It is through prayer that we are released into the power of praise because then our eyes are moved away from ourselves and even from our problem and are fixed instead on the greatness and goodness of God. Faith sees what God has done in Jesus. The secret of victory in spiritual warfare within our own experience is summed up in the words of the prophet to king Jehoshophat:

'Do not be afraid or discouraged because of this vast army. For the battle is not yours, but God's' (2 Chronicles 20.15).

3. The art of spiritual warfare

Spiritual warfare is not complicated but it is hard! There are a number of basic principles you should never forget:

(a) *The name of Jesus*

Time and again the New Testament writers stress the importance of the name of Jesus. Jesus is the Greek equivalent of the Old Testament word, Joshua, and means the same: 'deliverer' or 'saviour'. Jesus himself emphasised the importance of the name when he instructed his disciples to live in its power:

'I tell you the truth, anyone who has faith in me will do what I have been doing. He will do even greater things than these. ... You may ask for anything in my name, and I will do it' (John 14.12, 14).

Throughout the Acts of the Apostles we read of the followers of Jesus acting in the name of Jesus. When confronted by opposition and real danger it is with the name of Jesus that they invoke the Father:

'Stretch out your hand to heal and perform miraculous signs and wonders through the name of your holy servant Jesus' (Acts 4.30).

Paul urges his readers to do everything in the name of Jesus (Colossians 3.17).

When we pray in the name of Jesus, we are bringing into focus all that God has done and promised in Jesus. He has given to him 'the name that is above every name',

'that at the name of Jesus every knee should bow, in heaven and on earth and under the earth' (Philippians 2.10).

Satan recognises the power of Jesus and he knows that Jesus is the one who has secured his ultimate defeat. So the power we have is the power that belongs to the name of Jesus.

(b) *The fellowship of faith*

Anyone who engages in war is vulnerable. You cannot attack an enemy without the risk of being attacked yourself. Counter-attack is one of the great capabilities of Satan. Therefore it is important to be covered by the prayer and faith of other believers. The shield that was carried by the Roman infantryman was important because of how it was constructed. It was not a single skinned implement but had a number of layers. This meant that when fiery darts were thrown at the soldier they sank into the first layer or so and were extinguished. So it is with the fellowship of faith. By ourselves we are that much more vulnerable but as we stand together in faith there is the added protection of layers of faith.

The other important fact about fellowship in this battle is that faith builds faith. When the pressure is on, the encouragement of other Christians enables us to stand in the thick of the fight.

(c) *The power of the word*

We need to learn our language of faith. There are a number of ways in which to approach the Scriptures. One important way is at the level of discovering our faith-language. Take a coloured pencil and when a verse or passage comes alive in your heart and creates faith then mark it. When the Devil comes with doubt or you are engaged in a spiritual battle go back to your faith-language and use that in the fight.

Many times when I am praying with different people the Lord gives me a verse of Scripture for them in particular. That is not just a memory-verse, it is a word of faith specially addressed to them. They have to take it and allow it to become what it says within their experience.

That is the power of the word. It becomes what it says. Sadly, in the Church today, the confidence of many people in the power of the word of God has been undermined. To use it or quote it has become unfashionable and by some regarded as archaic and fundamentalist. Be that as it may, it has become my experience through the Holy Spirit that a word from Scripture has living power. To speak a word from God into a situation in this way means that we are delivered from the fear or need of dreaming up some appropriate word of our own. When God speaks, things happen!

(d) *The resources of the Holy Spirit*

The way we are equipped by the Spirit to undertake this battle of spiritual warfare is highlighted by James in his letter:

> 'If any of you lacks wisdom, *he should ask God*, who gives generously to all without finding fault' (James 1.5).

This is the secret of how all spiritual resources are obtained – on request! We need to come to the Father and ask him to provide us with the essentials for the battle. God will not leave us to fight the battle in our own strength because then we would lose before we started.

(e) *The effectiveness of prayer*

It is in the area of intercession in particular that prayer is effective in spiritual warfare. To be an intercessor is to make your heart and mind available to God. God's battles on earth are often fought within the spirits of those who spend time in intercessory prayer. Intercessory prayer is not just coming to God with requests, it is God writing the agenda of his purposes for the world on the hearts and minds of those who want to co-operate with him. That is why intercession involves such a real cost. There is pain at the heart of it because intercessors bear God's burdens for the world and the needs of the world within their own beings.

There is a deep mystery about this. It seems as though at those times when intercession is real to us, we can become very aware in our spirits of some of God's immediate concerns with the world.

Not very long ago a friend of mine was travelling across London. She was going to pay a social visit on some close friends. On her way she drove through a very run-down part of town with large areas of high-rise flats. The further she went the more burdened she became for the people who lived in that area and especially for the children. Through the whole evening she was quite pre-occupied in her spirit in prayer. It was almost as though the Holy Spirit had taken her behind the doors she had seen and had given her a first-hand experience of the problems and needs of some of those people. That burden remained with her the whole evening until about midnight, when it suddenly lifted. It was almost as though she heard God telling her that it was all right now. God had used her intercession in the mystery of his purpose in the spiritual struggle in heavenly places. She almost heard him saying to her, 'Mission accomplished!'

For some people this is not enough. They do not believe the prayer has been real unless they have discovered in detail how God has used it. It is not like that in the field of spiritual warfare. We may never know to what extent, or in exactly what way, our prayer prevailed in a given situation. It is enough that it is used!

The old Methodist preacher, Samuel Chadwick had no doubt about the effectiveness of prayer in the struggle with the powers of evil. He said,

'Satan dreads nothing but prayer ... activities are multiplied that meditation may be ousted, and organisations increased that prayer may have no chance. The one concern of the Devil is to keep the saints from praying. He fears nothing from prayerless studies, prayerless work, prayerless religion. He laughs at our toil, mocks at our wisdom, but trembles when we pray.'

It is amazing to think that a Christian can go on for years with little or no understanding of this whole area of spiritual experience. That was certainly true for me.

It is equally sad that many have shunted all thoughts about spiritual warfare into a siding for the weird and sinister when all the time it stands at the heart of all true Christian experience. We need to recognise that it is a battle we are all involved in through the power of the Holy Spirit. We need to learn the art of spiritual warfare and become confident through God of our ability to stand in his strength and overcome the power of the enemy. We need to take to ourselves the full armour of God:

> 'so that ... you may be able to stand your ground, and after you have done everything, to stand' (Ephesians 6.13).

9: Seeing is believing!

'I have been crucified with Christ and I no longer live, but Christ lives in me. The life I live in the body, I live by faith in the Son of God, who loved me and gave himself for me' (Galatians 2.20).

I was preaching in a small Baptist chapel in the south of England. It was the Wednesday of Holy Week and I had more or less determined on the theme for the talk that night. As I stood to speak my Bible fell open at Galatians chapter 2 and the words of verse 20 stood out like neon lights. Suddenly it hit me again: to be a Christian is to live life on a radically different basis from the normal run of human experience. The words of Paul hit me with very direct power:

'I live by faith in the Son of God.'

Faith is a response; it is what happens in my life when my eyes have been opened to just how much God has done for me in Jesus.

To live by faith is to live in absolute trust in God, to believe that he is able to bring the direction and the provision for everything that we need in every area of our Christian experience. Faith is not a cop-out, it is not the way to an easy buck, or the excuse to leave our employment and expect everything to fall from heaven. Faith is an attitude; it is a way of looking at life through God's eyes. Faith looks at everything I have and everything I am and asks how these things serve God's purpose here on earth.

Some people imagine that 'living by faith' does not really start until they have given up their job and have no longer any

139

visible means of support. That has had the effect of associating faith with money.

Faith is much more dynamic than that! It is the gift that God gives us to enable us to live our lives in his power. Faith is the channel through which God is able to pour his power into our lives. Faith operates at a level of experience and awareness that is closed to the normal range of human endeavour.

'Now faith is being sure of what we hope for and certain of what we do not see' (Hebrews 11.1).

Words like these have led some to believe that faith is blind. To say that faith *does not see* is quite different from saying that *faith cannot see*. Faith sees all right, but its eyes are focussed on a different set of realities from normal vision.

Time and again in the Old Testament that fact is demonstrated in the experience of the prophets.

'This is what the Sovereign Lord showed me: a basket of ripe fruit. "What do you see, Amos?" he asked.
"A basket of ripe fruit," I answered.
Then the Lord said to me, "The time is ripe for my people Israel; I will spare them no longer."'

It takes the eyesight of faith to see beyond and behind the obvious and to perceive what God is doing and saying in the middle of the events and circumstances of our daily lives. Faith sees the significance of things and it focuses its attention on the realities of God.

It is not that faith is not realistic. It faces the vastness of the problem squarely. Only naivety minimises immense things and makes light of them. Faith never makes light of a difficulty, it simply is not overwhelmed by it because it looks beyond and sees the vastness of God and his power.

At the heart of everything we have shared through this book stands this reality of faith. Renewal in faith is the key to almost every other experience within our Christian lives. For myself, faith used to operate at an intellectual level; it was something I believed in my mind. Faith was the set of propositions that, for me, made up the essence of the Christian gospel. Not that there is anything wrong with that – it just isn't enough!

A friend of mine, a Roman Catholic priest, once summed the issue up in a nutshell. He said, 'The longest journey in the world is from a man's head to his heart.'

I have discovered that faith is not just a set of beliefs, it is a dynamic principle of life. It is the means by which God releases all his power and realises a whole new world of spiritual potential for my inner life. That is why the writer to the Hebrews said:

'Without faith it is impossible to please God' (Hebrews 11.6).

Professor F. F. Bruce says in his commentary on Hebrews 11, the great chapter of faith:

'Physical eyesight produces conviction about visible things; faith is the organ which enables people (like Moses in v. 27) to see the invisible.'

1. The focus of faith

Faith does not work in thin air. Faith focuses into certain important facts. These are not facts that are appreciated at the level of normal human intuition. They are the sort of facts that are taught to us by the Holy Spirit. To all outward appearances Jesus was only another specially gifted human being with a tremendous capacity for love and goodness. Great men, like Gandhi, have made precisely that judgment about him. For them there is something magnificent about Jesus that is worthy of praise and respect, but that is not the view of faith.

Faith sees into the heart of the matter because it is not informed by the facts as they appear outwardly, it is taught by the Holy Spirit. When our eyes are opened in faith to the real truth about Jesus, we are living in the fulfillment of the very words of Jesus himself. Speaking of the work of the Holy Spirit he said:

'He will bring glory to me by taking from what is mine and making it known to you' (John 16.14).

Paul made the same claim about the work of the Holy Spirit

within human experience when he said to the Corinthians:

'We have not received the spirit of the world but the Spirit who is from God, that we may understand what God has freely given us' (1 Corinthians 2.12).

When the Holy Spirit works in our hearts, the first thing that happens is that our eyes are opened to the truth of God in Jesus.

An instance of this is described in the story of Stan Telchin, a Jew who discovered for himself the real significance of Jesus. He tells his story in his book, *Betrayed*. At one point he describes the difficulty he had with the truth of the Virgin Birth and how he talked about this with a Catholic actor friend.

'Come on Louis! I've got a lot of respect for you and for what you believe, but do you really believe that stuff about a virgin birth? You're not stupid. You know the facts of life. How can you believe that stuff?' Louis looked at me very seriously and said, 'I believe because I have the gift of faith.'

Stan Telchin goes on to reflect about what has happened since the Holy Spirit worked within his life. In his own words, 'Boy! If Louis could see me now!'

The Spirit fixes our eyes on some of the most important facts with regard to Jesus. His job is to make us realise just what a tremendous thing God has accomplished in Christ and just how important that is for our own living in the here and now. For example:

(a) *He teaches us the measure of God's provision*

Paul spells it out in Romans 8.32:

'He who did not spare his own Son, but gave him up for us all – how will he not also, along with him, graciously give us all things!'

The extent of God's provision in our lives is measured by

the fact that he has already made the ultimate provision in the death of Jesus.

Paul makes the point again in Philippians 4.19:

'And my God will meet all your needs according to his glorious riches in Christ Jesus.'

It is when our eyes have been opened to the sheer magnificence of God's love in Jesus that our faith is enabled to trust God for his provision in every other area of our lives. After Jesus, every other gift is merely a footnote!

(b) *He teaches us the measure of God's power*

There is a direct line drawn in the New Testament between what God has done in the experience of Jesus and what he does in the experience of the believer. This is a tremendous fact! Paul spells out its implications for us in Ephesians 1.19:

' . . . his incomparably great power for us who believe. That power is like the working of his mighty strength, which he exerted in Christ when he raised him from the dead and seated him at his right hand in the heavenly realms.'

That is what faith focuses on – not on the immensity of the problem, nor on the inadequacy of the individual, but on the mighty power of God that was at work in Jesus and is available to all who trust in God.

(c) *He teaches us the measure of God's promise*

Faith walks hand in hand with hope. By its very nature hope is something that is not immediately seen. As Paul says in Romans 8.24:

'For in this hope we were saved. But hope that is seen is not hope at all. Who hopes for what he already sees? But if we hope for what we do not yet have, we wait for it patiently.'

The vision of what God is taking us towards is the gift of the

143

Holy Spirit. The news of what God is going to do for us in Jesus is not something that is gleaned from the columns of the daily paper or the presenters of *News at Ten*. It comes from the witness of the Holy Spirit through the Scriptures and in our hearts. It is the fulfillment in us of the prayer of Paul:

'May the God of hope fill you with all joy and peace as you trust in him, *so that you may overflow with hope by the power of the Holy Spirit*' (Romans 15.13).

When we see, in faith, the hope of God's promise in Jesus it has a tremendous, liberating effect in our lives.

'Therefore we do not lose heart. Though outwardly we are wasting away, yet inwardly we are being renewed day by day. For our light and momentary troubles are achieving for us an eternal glory that far outweighs them all. *So we fix our eyes not on what is seen, but on what is unseen.* For what is seen is temporary, but what is unseen is eternal' (2 Corinthians 4.16–18).

Faith feeds on these spiritual realities. Apart from the work of the Spirit they are completely hidden to us. The Spirit replaces eyesight with a perception that enables faith to operate in the strength of the promises of God.

2. The dynamics of faith

Faith is released and increased within our lives by the operation of the gifts of the Holy Spirit. According to 1 Corinthians 12.9, faith is one of the special gifts of the Holy Spirit. Yet the gifts as a whole are the means by which faith operates in our lives. They are the dynamics of faith. Faith in action depends on the operation of the gifts of the Spirit. We can see what this means when we look at some of the gifts of the Spirit listed in 1 Corinthians 12.

(a) *The language of faith*

Tongues operate as the prayer-language of faith in the life of the Christian. There are many occasions and circumstances where we do not know what or how to pray. As we pray the Spirit enables our faith through the operation of the gift of tongues. God can speak his own language in us and so bring us into a position of faith.

This is particularly true in the realm of spiritual warfare, as we saw in the last chapter. We can address the powers of evil by the use of tongues in a way and strength that would be quite impossible within the limitations of our own tongue. Paul says that, 'He who speaks in a tongue edifies himself' (1 Corinthians 14.4).

We see the question of the gifts of the Holy Spirit in a completely new light when we begin to realise that they are not only given to improve our feelings about God, but they are essential for a full exercise of faith. Without a faith-language we are all too conscious of the weakness and limitations of our own speech. The language of the Holy Spirit through us liberates us into the power of God in prayer.

'In the same way, the Spirit helps us in our weakness. We do not know what we ought to pray, but the Spirit himself intercedes for us with groans that words cannot express' (Romans 8.26).

(b) *The understanding of faith*

'If any of you lacks wisdom, he should ask God, who gives generously to all without finding fault; and it will be given to you' (James 1.5).

Faith is certainly not blind when it comes to seeing how God views things. In fact, faith believes that God will impart his understanding into the situation and that the right word will be given to meet the circumstances in hand. I take it that wisdom in James 1.5 carries with it the thought that the Holy Spirit will provide the appropriate words of direction or advice to meet the need so that right action can follow. Such knowledge is incisive. It sees right into the heart of the matter and lays the whole situation bare before God and man. It opens the way up for God to deal with problems in the way he sees fit.

Faith claims the wisdom of God and works on the principle that God knows the heart and will reveal his understanding into the hand of faith.

(c) *The works of faith*

Faith, to be real, needs to issue in deeds. James says so:

'Faith by itself, if it is not accompanied by action, is dead' (James 2.17).

It is significant that a good number of the gifts of the Holy Spirit that are listed in Romans 12 and 1 Corinthians 12 are 'action-oriented' gifts. They enable God to act through our lives into the world. In 1 Corinthians the significant gifts in this area are the gifts of faith, healing and miracles. It is very easy for us to see the need for these practical gifts of the Spirit today when so many people are held in the grip of powerful spiritual forces, and when despair and a sense of hopelessness have caused so many to live in defeat. In spite of all our modern capabilities in the realm of chemotherapy and psychotherapy it becomes apparent time and again that there is need for supernatural ability to bring about healing in people's lives. This in no way by-passes, or detracts from, the importance of healing medicine and the skill of the physician. It extends it. It means that alongside the technical medical skill of the practitioner come the gifts of insight and knowledge that are the gift of the Spirit of God.

The fact of the matter, anyway, is that with all our skill we still frequently come to the end of ourselves. Then we are left with God! His power to work miracles is no more diminished today than it ever was.

The 'action-oriented' gifts of the Spirit described in Romans 12 urgently need to be recovered for the body of Christ today. The gift of service, for example, is that spiritual ability to give ourselves without reserve to the needs of others. When we are freed by the Holy Spirit into a new capacity for love and concern, the result far exceeds any effort we could have made in the power of our own flesh. Again, take the gift of contribution. Never was a gift more needed in the Church at large! This gift could be described as 'a God-given inclination to give'. It takes a special unction of the Holy Spirit to release us from small-mindedness in the area of our giving. When the Spirit opens our eyes to all that God has done, our own spirits are set free to use everything we have to the glory of God. That was the gift which was released at Pentecost. The hallmark of the young Church was:

'Selling their possessions and goods, they gave to anyone as he had need' (Acts 2.45).

Even the gifts of organisation and social concern are viewed in Romans 12 as special gifts of the Spirit. The fact is that our works of faith are not things we do to *earn* God's mercy, they are things we do because we have received God's mercy. They are not the means of grace, but are the result of grace.

Faith is put into action by means of the gifts the Holy Spirit brings into our lives. Without these gifts we are back trying to carry out God's work in our own strength.

(d) *The insight of faith*

Time and again the New Testament recognises that the life of faith is one that operates in a context of spiritual opposition. The Devil is a master-counterfeiter and he is able to produce language and actions that seem, to be godly. It takes a special eyesight of the Spirit to be able to look behind the scenes and perceive what is actually happening.

Wherever God is at work in the power of his Holy Spirit the Devil is highly active sowing confusion and pretence in an attempt to bring the work of God into disrepute. John warned his readers of the need for discernment when he said.

'Dear friends, do not believe every spirit, but test the spirits whether they are from God' (1 John 4.1).

He goes on to offer some criteria against which the claims can be tested. Chiefly, of course, a person's words must be tested by what he says about Jesus. Jesus is the ultimate standard, as far as the New Testament is concerned, of any claim that is made to divine revelation. It is not surprising to note, therefore, how relevant that particular test is with regard to many modern heretical movements. On the surface it seems almost naive to say that you can test a spirit by its response to Jesus. Yet history bears out the fact that time and again it is just here that false teaching, both inside and outside the historic churches, has shown its hand.

In 1 Corinthians 12 Paul speaks of the gift of discernment, 'the ability to distinguish between spirits' (1 Corinthians 12.10). This gift is not so much the knowledge of right doctrine against which to test the claims that are being made, so much as the immediate ability that is given by the Holy Spirit to be able to discern what is taking place deep within the recesses of a person's being, or see what the Devil is getting up to in a particular situation.

Paul himself was aware of the continual need for discernment, even in his dealings with fellow believers in the churches to which he wrote. His actions were often designed to thwart Satan's evil attempts to divide and spoil the witness of the young Christians. Paul knew the need for the eyesight of faith:

'For we are not unaware of his schemes'
(2 Corinthians 2.11).

This study of the gifts of the Holy Spirit in relation to faith highlights for us just how important it is to live in the power and reality of these gifts. We cannot really live a life of faith in the fullest sense unless we live in the gifts of the Holy Spirit. This releases these gifts from being an option open to a few Christians who are inclined that way, to becoming an absolute necessity in the life of every Christian believer and church. For as the late A. W. Tozer says in his book *Keys to the Deeper Life*:-

'Religious work can be done by natural men without the gifts of the Spirit, and it can be done well and skilfully. But work designed for eternity can only be done by the eternal Spirit. No work has eternity in it unless it is done by the Spirit through the gifts he has himself implanted in the souls of redeemed men.'

3. The test of faith

It is remarkable but true that where the Scriptures say most about faith, they say it in a context of suffering and testing. The ultimate confession of faith in the Scriptures is summed up in the words of the Psalmist:

'Praise our God, O peoples,
let the sound of his praise be heard;
he has preserved our lives

and kept our feet from slipping.
For you, O God, tested us;
you refined us like silver.
You brought us into prison
and laid burdens on our backs.
You let men ride over our heads;
we went through fire and water,
but you brought us to a place of abundance'
(Psalm 66.8–12).

It is of the nature of faith that it endures testing. We need to recognise this as a principle of the life of faith. To live by faith is to be open to the testing of that faith under the hand of God. Peter puts it like this:

'In this you greatly rejoice, though now for a little while you may have had to suffer grief in all kinds of trials. These have come so that your faith – of greater worth than gold, which perishes even though refined by fire – may be proved genuine and may result in praise, glory and honour when Jesus Christ is revealed'
(1 Peter 1.6, 7).

There are a number of ways in which faith will be tested.

(a) *Through silence*

It is a fact of experience that often when we stand in faith for a particular project or concern, it seems, in the period that immediately follows, as though the heavens are like brass. James highlights the result of this:

'You know that the testing of your faith develops perseverance' (James 1.3).

If we decide to live by faith, then we will come to know first-hand the agony of the Psalmist when he cried in anguish:

'My God, my God, why have you forsaken me?
Why are you so far from saving me,
so far from the words of my groaning?' (Psalm 22.1).

This is a *purifying* silence. In it we come to know every detail of our inner heart, our reactions and responses, and quite often we see just how unbelieving we really are. Yet it is this silence of God that saves us from acting as though faith were magic, as though we had merely to wave a wand to make what we wanted or believed was right fall from heaven.

This is a *refining* silence. Within the silences of God our vision is re-adjusted. There our dreams are tested and what is only vain imagination falls away into oblivion. When God breaks the silence we discover that he had heard us before we even spoke and he had used the silence creatively to bring us into his will:

> 'Before they call I will answer; while they are still speaking I will hear' (Isaiah 65.24).

(b) *Through turmoil*

The most intense moments of spiritual warfare are often experienced with the exercise of faith. It is when we have come to God with our vision and have laid it before him in praying faith that doubt and warfare become the facts of our existence.

The Devil seeks to batter us into submission and defeat. Faith is his greatest enemy and therefore all his vengeance is directed towards the believing heart. That is why the greatest men and women of faith have known most about the reality of spiritual warfare.

God permits this so that we may develop toughness. Faith does not wilt under this onslaught but uses it as a training course for the work of the Kingdom. Faith redeems what could be a negative experience and makes it good for the service of God. Faith does not look at the ferocity of the Devil's attack but at the promise of God.

> 'God is faithful; he will not let you be tempted beyond what you can bear. But when you are tempted, he will also provide a way out so that you can stand up under it' (1 Corinthians 10.13).

(c) *Through suffering*

The further we go the more the mystery deepens. It is

Hebrews 11, the greatest faith-chapter in the Bible, that exposes the deepest truth about faith. That great catalogue of faith soars through all the known heroes of faith in Old Testament times until it reaches its crescendo in the anonymous witness of those saints who suffered unimaginable torture for the sake of their faith in Christ.

'They were stoned; they were sawed in two; they were put to death by the sword. They went about in sheepskins and goatskins, destitute, persecuted and ill-treated – *the world was not worthy of them*'
(Hebrews 11.37, 38).

What a different picture from some of our modern triumphalist versions of faith! How can we ever explain this?

It was through suffering that God himself chose to redeem the world:

'Who for the joy set before him endured the cross, scorning its shame, and sat down at the right hand of the throne of God' (Hebrews 12.2).

It is not that suffering is the will of God for us. Yet the eye of faith can perceive when suffering is to be the means by which God will release his power into the lives of other people. There is no virtue in suffering for suffering's sake, there is only meaning in it when God takes it, and through faith, makes it the vehicle of redemption for others.

'We have this treasure in jars of clay to show that this all-surpassing power is from God and not from us'
(2 Corinthians 4.7).

4. The exercise of faith

In his book, *Anything You Ask*, my colleague Colin Urquhart, has dealt expansively with the life of faith:

'We modern people like to deal with facts. Present us with a set of facts and we know where we stand. We have become very suspicious of promises. We are too familiar with politicians who make enticing statements, which are at best fond hopes; at worst, deliberate deception. ... God, however, has chosen to work in the lives of his people, by asking them to believe a series of promises that he gives them. But he is no human politician, or well-meaning, but unreliable parent. By contrast, he is faithful to his Word – always!'

There are certain important principles that we must take to heart if our faith is to grow and mature:

(a) *Faith comes by hearing*

What creates faith within our hearts is the creative word of God. Unless God had spoken to us in the power of his Spirit we would never have responded in trust.

'Faith comes from hearing the message, and the message is heard through the word of Christ' (Romans 10.17).

To live effectively by faith we need always to be living under the power of the word of God. When God speaks, something always happens. This is why it is important for us to live in submission to the word of God through the Scriptures. This is the primary means of the revelation of God's word to us and when that word is allowed to take root the result is faith.

Take a coloured pencil and underline your faith-language in the Scriptures. Whenever you read your Bible take note of those passages and verses by which the Spirit creates faith in your heart. Note them and keep going back to them particularly in times of battle or difficulty and allow the word to bring faith to life within your heart.

In his confrontation with the Devil, Jesus himself stressed the importance of the word of God in our lives.

'Jesus answered, "It is written: 'Man does not live on bread alone, but on every word that comes from the mouth of God'"' (Matthew 4.4).

The Holy Spirit wants to make the Bible live for us in a powerful way. It is the food of faith. Faith lives on the word!

(b) *Faith advances by walking*

Faith doesn't stand still! Faith moves from one point of trust to the next. It is just like using your legs. You can either stand still with your feet together, or you can put one foot out in front of the other and go somewhere! If you stand with your feet together you will be perfectly balanced, but you will go nowhere. To take a step is to take the risk of imbalance. As soon as you put one foot in front of the other you are in a state of imbalance, but you are on the move!

Faith is the footstep of the believer. The logic of taking one step of faith is that you will need to take another. It is of the nature of faith that it is always looking for the next step. Faith never arrives, at least not in this life.

(c) *Faith matures by waiting*

This is not a contradiction to what has just been said. This is no passive waiting. Colin Urquhart puts it like this:

'Faith is a continuous attitude of believing until the answer is seen.'

James puts it like this:

'You know that the testing of your faith develops perseverance' (James 1.3).

Some time ago we were praying for specific needs within our household. We had been praying for a few days and still the answer hadn't arrived. On one particular morning we began to thank God in advance for what he was doing. A vivid picture came to my mind. It was the picture of the man who is described in Psalm 1.

'He is like a tree planted by streams of water,
which yields its fruit in season
and whose leaf does not wither' (Psalm 1.3).

It suddenly dawned on us that the picture fitted our situation. It was as though we were being confirmed in our life in God: our leaves were green! We were waiting for the fruit to appear. That experience brought a great sensation of elation and strength. We knew there was a purpose in the waiting and that through it our faith was being strengthened.

(d) *Faith receives by asking*

It is important to be specific in prayer. Time and again Jesus encouraged his disciples to be definite in their prayers. Faith grows when we get into clear focus what it is that we are praying for or about. Sometimes we have difficulty in the area of answered prayer because we are never quite sure what the question was.

Specific asking develops our faith in God.

'When he asks, he must believe and not doubt, because he who doubts is like a wave of the sea, blown and tossed by the wind. That man should not think he will receive anything from the Lord; he is a double-minded man, unstable in all he does' (James 1.6, 7).

It is in the process of asking that we discover God's will. That is why there is often waiting or some test connected with a prayer of request or intercession. It is not that God hasn't heard our cry. It is that it takes him some time to get us to ask the right question. Often in our time of waiting and testing we will find that our perception of the question will change. Our minds will become aware of the mind of God in the matter and it may be that our desires and requests will change radically.

This is where the work of the Holy Spirit is so important to us as we pray. We need to learn to pray 'in the Spirit' (Ephesians 6.18). Paul makes it clear in Romans 8.26 that when we are uncertain what to pray for the Holy Spirit is there to point us in the right direction to find the will of God.

This is where, also, the gift of tongues is so vitally important. As we are moved to pray in tongues so we are led into an awareness of what we should be praying about in particular. When we enter into the heart of a specific request then we know how to look for a specific answer.

(e) *Faith wins by persisting*

This is another area in which Jesus was quite specific. He

taught his disciples the need to be persistent in prayer.

'Then Jesus told his disciples a parable to show them
that they should always pray and not give up'
(Luke 18.1).

Apart from the fact that pertinacity demonstrates the
character of our faith there are other, more serious reasons
why we should persist in prayer. S. D. Gordon stresses this:

'Prayer is insisting upon Jesus' victory, and the retreat
of the enemy on each particular spot. The enemy yields
only what he must. He yields only what is taken.
Therefore ground must be taken step by step. Prayer
must be definite.'

We are engaged in a cosmic struggle. Faith operates in the
arena of spiritual warfare. It is through the insistence of faith
that territory is going to be regained from the enemy.

'This is the victory that has overcome the world, even
our faith. Who is he that overcomes the world? Only he
who believes that Jesus is the Son of God'
(1 John 5.4, 5).

5. The goal of faith

'Though you have not seen him, you love him; and
even though you do not see him now, you believe in
him and are filled with an inexpressible and glorious
joy, for you are receiving the goal of your faith, the
salvation of your souls' (1 Peter 1.8, 9).

Everything we are involved in through faith points
forward. Faith operates in the here and now but it lives in the
light of the there and then!

Through the power of faith we see the evidence of God at
work today but even that carries within it the promise of all
that God is going to do tomorrow. Pentecost was founded on
hope:

'Men of Galilee why do you stand here looking into the

sky? This same Jesus, who has been taken from you into heaven, will come back in the same way you have seen him go into heaven' (Acts 1.11).

Faith meets our daily needs. Faith enables us to know the victory of Jesus in the daily struggle with the powers of evil. Yet ultimately faith goes beyond all these things. It transcends the mortal, it extends beyond the finite. Faith locks itself into the reality of the eternal kingdom where death and the curse hold no more sway. The ultimate goal of faith is that kingdom where only the righteousness of God will prevail.

'I declare to you, brothers, that flesh and blood cannot inherit the kingdom of God, nor does the perishable inherit the imperishable. ... For the perishable must clothe itself with the imperishable, and the mortal with immortality ... then the saying that was written will come true: "Death has been swallowed up in victory"' (1 Corinthians 15.50, 53, 54).

This is not a vague, life-evading hope. If you look in the pages of the New Testament you will find that this hope is the source of the most dynamic and practical action the world has ever known. People who live within this perspective of faith are set free from the fears and concerns that bind most of us to the things of time and sense. To live in the power of faith as it looks ahead into God's tomorrow is to know the buoyancy of Spirit that comes from a deep sense of expectation:

'Therefore we do not lose heart. Though outwardly we are wasting away, yet inwardly we are being renewed day by day. ... So we fix our eyes not on what is seen, but on what is unseen. For what is seen is temporary, but what is unseen is eternal' (2 Corinthians 4.16, 18).

This hope is at the very centre of our new life through the Spirit of Jesus. To live in the power of the Holy Spirit is to participate in the hope of Jesus.

'Praise be to the God and Father of our Lord Jesus Christ! In his great mercy he has given us new birth into a living hope through the resurrection of Jesus Christ from the dead, and into an inheritance that can never perish, spoil or fade – kept in heaven for you, who through faith are shielded by God's power until the coming of the salvation that is ready to be revealed in the last time' (1 Peter 1.3–5).

This book has become a journal of faith. Faith has become the most exciting venture of my life. God wants us all to live by faith. There is no other way to live as a Christian: it is the only way that God can fulfill his purpose through us and it is the only way that we can enter into our full inheritance as sons and daughters of the Kingdom. When we learn to live by faith we will see the power of God released through our lives to a degree that we never imagined possible.

'Therefore, since we are surrounded by such a great cloud of witnesses, let us throw off everything that hinders, and the sin that so easily entangles, and let us run with perseverance the race marked out for us. Let us fix our eyes on Jesus, the author and perfector of our faith, who for the joy set before him endured the cross, scorning its shame, and sat down on the right hand of the throne of God' (Hebrews 12.1, 2).